AWAKENING

The Upside of Y2K

AWAKENING

The Upside of Y2K

Edited by Judy Laddon,

Tom Atlee & Larry Shook

THE PRINTED WORD

ISBN 0-9667030-0-6 (pbk.)

Additional copies of this book can be obtained by sending checks or money orders, $10 per book, plus $2 postage and handling, with shipping information to: The Printed Word, 4327 S. Perry, Spokane, WA 99203, USA. Volume discounts available. Call (509) 624-3177.

Printed in the United States of America.
First printing August 1998

The grief you cry out from
draws you toward union.
Your pure sadness
that wants help
is the secret cup.

Listen to the moan of a dog for its master.
That whining is the connection [to the Divine].

There are love dogs
no one knows the names of.

Give your life
to be one of them.

—*Rumi*

For Dorothy Shook,
who has known hard times
and who has loved all the children
all her life

CONTENTS

Introduction

PRETEND SOMEONE invented a new game. Like using an ordinary deck of playing cards, you can play by yourself or with others. When you're first introduced to the game, though, you're alone. It's solitaire. The instructions:

#1. Begin with a scenario: you have just discovered that the world as you know it is about to change drastically. The way you live, how you heat your house, acquire your food and clothing, the manner in which you travel from point A to point B in your town or city, the way you expect water to flow from the tap, how you find entertainment, how money arrives in your pocket, what you do at work, all these things that you have come to rely upon as certain as the sun rising each morning come crashing to a halt.

Your mission, should you choose to proceed with this game, is to select from the following list of responses:

A) No response. In the time lag between this moment and the fast-approaching moment of truth, you ignore the mission. (1 Player. Game's over. Put the cards away.)

B) Confusion. You spread word of the coming chaos, tear your hair, cry with friends and family, encourage misery in others, and take no real action. (This works best with from 1 to 20 players.)

C) Panic. This selection is characterized by massive activity and is especially effective in groups. Possibilities: withdraw all your money from banks and investments; move to the country with some like-minded friends and set up concertina wire around your compound; stock your basement with a huge stash of food; train your doberman to attack; cache 10-years' extra ammo for your guns; publish pamphlets announcing that God prefers your group, and predict that everyone else will die. (Suggested: 4 to 40 players. Families preferred.)

D) Spiritual Awakening. Greet this mission as a quirky, crazy answer to an unspoken prayer. If you've been wanting to live a simpler life, aching to spend more time with your family, wanting a closer relation to the Creator (whatever your belief system), yearning to find ways to have a gentler impact on the earth, if you've wanted to have a community of friends who mutually support one another, tell stories in the evening, shell peas together, then proceed to

#2. (To be continued...)
The name of the game: "Y2K."

THE FIRST TIME I heard of Y2K it sounded like gibberish. The man speaking the words was a noted futurist, Robert Theobald, who had recently returned to Spokane to fight esophageal cancer with the support of long-time friends. Although in his 70s and weakened from his illness, Robert had recently received an infusion of funds and interest in his consulting work.

I had set up a meeting on the recommendation of a newspaper editor and writer friend of mine, Michael Guilfoil. I hadn't seen Michael for many months when I ran into him at Costco in early May 1998. I was glad to see him, because I wanted to tell him about my new job doing communications work for the Environmental Forum for Business, a nonprofit that puts on an annual conference.

As we stood in the bustling main aisle of the discount warehouse, determined shoppers were forced to push their carts around us; we moved to a side aisle for quieter interaction. Michael and I both became animated by the conversation. Looking at this youthfully handsome man in his early 40s, his graying hair no longer fashioned in the ponytail he once wore, I reflected how Michael has exerted a quiet influence in Spokane with what I consider enlightened feature reporting.

We both were obviously busy; a big cake box angled out of his cart—he was buying groceries for a birthday dinner for his wife—so we parted with the understanding we'd keep in touch. Sixty seconds later, as I reached for a sack of shelled walnuts, he came up behind me and called my name. "I have another thought," he said, and proceeded to tell me that I *had* to set up a meeting with Robert Theobald.

So I sat in the meeting room at the Spokane Intercollegiate Research and Technology Institute (SIRTI), where I work, along with my colleague, EFB's effevescent director, Lucy Gurnea, plus Bob Stilger, an EFB board member and close friend to Robert Theobald, Theobald himself and Michael Guilfoil.

The hour-long meeting didn't seem especially useful to me, much as I liked everyone in the room, coupled with the vista of the serene beauty of the Spokane River flowing outside the window. Robert Theobald kept referring to "Y2K," which I eventually understood had something to do with the computer date glitch recently mentioned in the news. He commented that he thought our forum needed some kind of unifying identity, and the others agreed. The forum's seven tracks—alternative energy, business, river restoration, higher education, socially responsible investing, design and construction, and the EPA's Sustainable Development Challenge Grant program—seemed to them scattered. Robert Theobald talked on about Y2K and the need for social "resilience."

Michael Guilfoil and I were the last to leave. "Robert's got kind of a *thing* about Y2K," he said, almost apologetically. The idea that a futurist, especially one who was staring into the maw of cancer, should become obsessed with some farfetched worry over the absence of two digits in a few computers seemed quaint and somehow pitiful to me. I didn't think much more about it.

Two weeks later, however, I got a phone call from my dear friend Sally Pierone. In the last twenty years Sally has established herself as a guru of a kind of New Age, self-help, personal growth network, an evolving, amorphous group of people, mostly women, seeking wisdom and guidance. And simple comfort. Still a beauty at age 77, full-figured with piercing, kindly blue eyes, Sally presents an ideal Mother archetype to women my age (I'm 50). (I'd been coming to Sally's house almost weekly for 12 years to attend women's discussion groups. In the beginning, at the time of the Harmonic Convergence in 1987, we were called "The Rolling Crones." Now it was the Meditation Group.)

"Judy, dear," Sally's voice intoned brightly, "I've invited Robert Theobald to come to Meditation on the 25th. I was hoping you would introduce him." Someone had suggested she invite him, she told me, and he had agreed to come; what did I think about it?

To myself I thought, well, he's a trifle conventional for our group, maybe a bit academic, with his British accent and his aura of having a national reputation. He'll probably want to talk about Y2K. Ho hum. To Sally I tried to inject a tone of convincing encouragement. "I'm sure he'll be great. That's a good idea, Sally. And of course, I'll be happy to introduce him. It just so happens I had a meeting with him not two weeks ago." A copy of an article listing his credits was sitting on my desk as we spoke.

So a month after my first meeting with him, there I was watching Robert Theobald in Sally's living room, gesturing gracefully with a ropy-veined hand, speaking to the assembled dozen or so women in a reasoned but somewhat urgent voice, describing the dangers of Y2K. By now I had figured out what the gibberish meant: Year Two Thousand. The computer glitch, the Millennial Bug.

The gathering expressed interest and curiosity. What should we do? We're always asking such questions, but they're couched in the realities of trying to juggle all the other complicated variables of our lives. I interpreted his answer as vague. Talk to your friends. Convene discussion groups in your home. Meet your neighbors and make lists of neighborhood resources. Start networking. I considered these suggestions in my own mind and quickly discarded them. I've got enough to do already, I thought. Plus I'm sure he doesn't understand the power of the group he's talking to.

But there I was wrong. He wanted to hear about our meetings, and he expressed polite but obviously intense interest in our shamanic journeys. When the presentation drew to an end and women stood up for the closing circle, Sally waved for Robert to get in the middle. We all gathered around him, touching one another and putting our hands on his tweed sports jacket, his leonine, graying head rising above us all. We spoke of our visions for a peaceful and abundant world, we blessed Robert himself and called for his healing, and we "toned," making a kind of tuneless moaning that moved into an almost angelic harmony that crescendoed into abrupt silence.

Still in the center of the circle, clearly moved, Robert reached a long arm around one or two women, giving hugs, smiling boyishly.

I purchased his latest book, *Reworking Success,* handing him a ten-dollar-bill that I didn't really want to part with. I brought the book home and promptly lost it.

A couple of weeks later Bob Stilger, Robert's good friend and a member of the five-person board of directors of the Environmental Forum for Business, walked into a board meeting and came right up to me. I found myself giving him a hug (he's the one board member I knew in a previous life, almost two decades ago, when my husband and I published *Spokane Magazine).* As Lucy Gurnea spread out sandwich makings, and the others served themselves coffee and socialized in twos and threes, Bob and I talked.

I don't remember the segue, but at one point I said, "What about this Y2K, Bob? What do you think of it? It is for real?" Yes, he said, it was for real. He had been working on it for some time, having meetings with others in the community, apparently not really moving anywhere with it. He had come to admit to himelf that he needed to protect his own personal energy. He added, "There's an article by Meg Wheatley and some other people that's the best I've seen on the issue." Having worked with a management consultant for several years, I recognized her name as a respected professional. I wanted to see it, I told him. Would he e-mail me the web site where I could find it?

The next day—after I read the article entitled, "The Year 2000: Social Chaos or Social Transformation?"—marked the beginning of my conversion. Something shifted in me and the clock started ticking. I found myself waking up in pre-dawn hours, my mind racing with ideas, suffused by an uncanny sense of purpose. It was as though my entire life had been created for this one moment, this one task before me.

For the three months I had worked at the Environmental Forum, Lucy Gurnea and I had been remarking on the sense of a divine hand at work. Resources seemed to show up before we knew we needed them. A banker called *us* to see if we needed a loan. National-class speakers were pleased to appear at this little conference in Spokane, Washington, at the end of October 1998. Doors opened. I remember writing an e-mail in response to a board member's expression of worry about uncertain revenues (in a conference, you have to spend a lot on promotion and printing before exhibiting and attendee revenues start to flow). "I'm sensing a baseball diamond in a corn field," I wrote, remembering the line, "Build it and they will come," from the movie *Field of Dreams* where history's baseball greats appear in the flesh from the netherworld.

Now, suddenly, it occurred to me the conference should address Y2K. That we had a remarkable opportunity—a framework already set up for public discussion about crucial areas of public sustenance: alternative energy, sustainable development, investing, water quality, the role of business. I had another idea: within four days I had mapped in my mind a plan for producing two books.

This first one, the volume you hold in your hand, is a collection of the best thinking I could find and/or commission about the problems and challenges of Y2K. As an editor, I knew instantly that such a book could be produced almost overnight. The theme would be responding to Y2K with what we know about sustainable living. Important threads of exploration into sustainable living date back to the '70s and '80s. I know this firsthand because, after our magazine went out of business in 1982, my husband Larry Shook and I entered what we affectionately call our homesteading phase. Though we live in town, we raised chickens and planted an organic garden; I made hard cheeses—painted with red wax and aged for six months—tofu from scratch, bread, canned fruit, pottery, hand-knit wool sweaters, etc. It was one of the most enjoyable periods of our lives, and we accumulated a library of resources and information.

Similarly, on the issue of, "Why worry about Y2K?" a lot of thinking and writing has already been done. For some reason, however, despite frank stories in *Newsweek* and other mainstream media, the fullness of the issue hasn't entered the national consciousness. When it does, it will be most constructive if it's framed in a certain way.

This book will not delve into the technicalities of computer programming and the frenetic corrective measures that are going on all over the world. I am trusting the analysis of others who know better than I the agonizing and shocking conclusion: there is no technical fix for this. Our response needs to go beyond technology. Beyond what we know. Beyond our faith in our own skills and powers of reason. We are entering a surreal world of no time, of powerlessness, of surrender. Despite the card game metaphor at the beginning of this introduction, we really have only two choices...

—*Judy Laddon*

Judy Laddon became aware of the seriousness of Y2K in the course of her work as Communications Director for the Environmental Forum for Business, a national conference taking place October 20-22, 1998, and September 20-22, 1999, in Spokane, Washington (Environmental Forum for Business, 665 N. Riverpoint, Ste 113, Spokane, WA 99202, 509-358-2073, enviro@sirti.org, www.environmentalforum.org).

Former co-publisher of *Spokane Magazine* and a staffer with *San Diego Magazine,* Ms. Laddon has been invoved in writing, editing and publishing for 25 years. She has edited numerous books and articles and has had a communications consulting practice for 15 years.

Is This Y2K Problem for Real?

BY TOM ATLEE

The simple answer is yes. Corporations and governments wouldn't be spending billions of dollars on it if it weren't real. But will it be a real crisis? There are two answers to that:
1. We don't know. And we won't know until it happens. There are just too many variables to make dependable predictions.
2. How much of a crisis it ends up being will depend on how much remediation and preparation we do beforehand — as individuals, organizations, communities and nations — and how wise we are about our choices. The more effective attention we put on this problem, the less of a problem it will prove to be.

But (you may well ask) how should we act NOW? This is the hard question. The longer we wait to find out how bad it's going to be, the less time we will have to prepare if it looks like a real crisis is inevitable. But preparation uses up precious time, attention and resources that we'd really like to use on other things right now. So we are faced with having to make judgements about how much preparation is wise, and when to start. Different people, groups, communities, organizations and countries will come to different conclusions. Time will tell whose judgements were wisest.

Personally, I think there is a real crisis unfolding which can only be ameliorated by *a lot* of us acknowledging that it is happening and putting *a lot* of attention on preparations. What follows is some of the evidence I have seen that led me to take this problem seriously.

THE INFORMED JUDGEMENTS OF AUTHORITIES

"I came here today because I wanted to stress the urgency of the challenge.... Clearly, we must set forth what the government is doing, what business is doing, but also what all of us have yet to do to meet this challenge together. And there is still a pressing need for action.... In the business sector just as in the government sector, there are still gaping holes. Far too many businesses, especially small- and medium-sized firms, will not be ready unless they begin to act. A recent Wells Fargo Bank survey shows that of the small businesses that even know about the problem, roughly half intend to do nothing

The Upside of Y2K 13

about it."
— PRESIDENT BILL CLINTON
In a speech about Y2K at the National Academy of Sciences, July 15, 1998

"I am very, very concerned that even as government and business leaders are finally acknowledging the seriousness of this problem, they are not thinking about the contingency plans that need to be put into place to minimize the harm from widespread failures.... I think we're no longer at the point of asking whether or not there will be any power disruptions, but we are now forced to ask how severe the disruptions are going to be.... If the critical industries and government agencies don't start to pick up the pace of dealing with this problem right now, Congress and the Clinton Administration are going to have to... deal with a true national emergency."
—SENATOR CHRISTOPHER J. DODD *(Democrat from Connecticut), at the first hearings of the Senate Special Committee on the Year 2000 Technology Problem, June 12, 1998*

"When people say to me, 'Is the world going to come to an end?' I say, 'I don't know.' I don't know whether this will be a bump in the road — that's the most optimistic assessment of what we've got, a fairly serious bump in the road — or whether this will, in fact, trigger a major worldwide recession with absolutely devastating economic consequences in some parts of the world... We must coldly, calculatingly divide up the next 18 months to determine what we can do, what we can't do, do what we can, and then provide for contingency plans for that which we cannot."
—SENATOR ROBERT F. BENNETT *(Republican from Utah), chair of the Senate Special Committee on the Year 2000 Technology Problem, in a speech June 2, 1998, to The Center for Strategic and International Studies.*

"The nation's utilities told a Senate panel today [June 12] that they were working to solve expected computer problems when 1999 ends but that they could not guarantee that the lights would not go out on Jan. 1, 2000."
—*New York Times, June 13, 1998*

The Electric Power Research Institute (EPRI) — a trade association for electric utility companies — says the Y2K problem will begin to disrupt businesses, including electric utilities, a year before the new century begins: "Major disruptions in technical and business operations could begin as early as January 1, 1999. Nearly every industry will be affected." [http://year2000.epriweb.com/year2000/ challenge.html]

Y2K is "the biggest screwup of the computer age" and it may cost $1 trillion to fix. [For comparison, the Vietnam War cost half that much, $500 billion.]
—GENE BYLINSKY, *"Industry Wakes Up to the Year 2000 Menace,"* **Fortune**, *April 27, 1998, pgs. 163-180. [http://www.pathfinder.com/fortune/1998/980427/imt.html]*

Y2K is a "very, very serious problem.... There's no point in sugar-coating the problem... If we don't fix the century-date problem, we will have a situation scarier than the average disaster movie you might see on a Sunday night."
—CHARLES ROSSETTI, COMMISSIONER OF THE U.S. INTERNAL REVENUE SERVICE (IRS), *cited by Tom Herman in "A Special Summary and Forecast of Federal and State Tax Developments,"* The Wall Street Journal, *April 22, 1998, pg. A1.*

"Serious vulnerabilities remain in addressing the federal government's Year 2000 readiness, and ... much more action is needed to ensure that federal agencies satisfactorily mitigate Year 2000 risks to avoid debilitating consequences.... As a result of federal agencies' slow progress, the public faces the risk that critical services could be severely disrupted by the Year 2000 computing crisis... Unless progress improves dramatically, a substantial number of mission-critical systems will not be year-2000 compliant in time."
—JOEL C. WILLEMSSEN in the GOVERNMENT ACCOUNTING OFFICE *report "Year 2000 Computing Crisis: Actions Must be Taken Now to Address the Slow Pace of Federal Progress" [GAO/T-AIMD-98-205] (Washington, D.C.: General Accounting Office, June 10, 1998). [http://www.gao.gov/y2kr.htm]*

"The focus of conversation among those best versed in this issue is about how we are going to clean up after what appears now to be an inevitable train wreck. As a society, we are on the point of conceding failure. Those unwilling or unable to move off the track are numerous. Federal agencies. State governments. Local and municipal governments. School districts. Private sector industries. Small and mid-sized companies. Critical infrastructure players. And most foreign nations. It's crazy. It's frustrating. It cannot be happening. But it is. Now the 'smart' questions have shifted to concentrate on contingency planning, crisis management, and liability. Lawyers are circling, and that is not a good sign. Failure is not part of the American fiber. Yet after this transition to the new century, society may have to admit that here was a situation it saw coming. Everyone understood its hard deadline. Everyone appreciated its worldwide scope. Everyone realized its massive potential to cause harm. And everyone let it happen. Given where the federal government stands today, I feel very confident in predicting that some mission-critical government systems will fail — perhaps as early as January 1, 1999. A recent ITAA survey showed that 44% of organizations have already experienced a Y2K failure."

—HARRIS N. MILLER, PRESIDENT OF INFORMATION TECHNOLOGY ASSOCIATION OF AMERICA *(ITAA), a trade association representing 11,000 information technology companies, testifying to the House Subcommittee on Oversight, Ways and Means Committee, May 7, 1998.*

"I plead guilty to journalistic incompetence for ignoring what may be one of the decade's big stories: the Year 2000 problem.... The House subcommittee on government management, information and technology, chaired by Rep. Stephen Horn (R-Calif.), estimates that the federal government has almost 8,000 'mission critical' computer systems and that only 35 percent are now prepared for the year 2000. At the present rate, the committee projects that only 63 percent will make it. Most disturbing is the estimate that only about a quarter of the Defense Department's 2,900 systems are now ready. Among private companies, readiness also seems spotty. The head of General Motors' information systems recently told *Fortune* magazine that the company is working feverishly to rectify 'catastrophic problems' at its plants.... The FAA reports that its radar has a date mechanism to regulate a critical coolant. If the software isn't fixed, 'the cooling system will not turn on at the correct time ... and the [radar] could overheat and shut down.' Potential glitches like this abound. No one knows how many there are. Millions of lines of software have to be scanned and, if wrong, rewritten, computers must then be tested.... Little testing has been done. It's complex and time-consuming. Often, systems can only be tested on weekends when not in use. For the press, I grasp the difficulties of covering this story. It's mostly hypothetical....[so] anyone writing about it now is shoved uneasily toward one of two polar positions: reassuring complacency (fixes will be made); or hysterical alarmism (the world will collapse).... I lean towards alarmism simply because all the specialists I contacted last week — people actually involved with fixing the computers — are alarmed. On the record, they say the problem is serious and the hour is late. Their cheeriest view is that 'no one knows' what will happen. Off the record, they incline toward Doomsday.... We can deny the possibilities and pray they don't materialize. Or we can pay attention and hope to minimize them. Either way, the year 2000 won't wait."

—ROBERT J. SAMUELSON, *"Computer Doomsday?"* **Washington Post,** *May 6, 1998*

"I would like to tell you that... the efforts of hundreds of Y2K-focused consulting firms around the world has pretty much worked, and that long before we hit the Y2K wall less than two years from now, the problems will be pretty much solved. I would like to tell you that— but it would be a lie.... Many, many firms, including some surprisingly large ones, have continued to drag their feet... and now won't possibly be ready to avoid disastrous problems come that cold January morning. For one thing, virtually everyone competent in the Y2K analysis-and-fixes business is already fully booked through January 1, 2000 and beyond. Companies with Y2K problems often cannot find people to work on those problems. Not just *enough* people, but *any* people.... The Y2K business ... is full of misinformation, hype, fear-mongering and exaggeration. Certainly some of that is crass, self-promoting hype by such entities as consulting and pro-gramming shops, which stand to benefit from spreading fear about Y2K meltdowns. But a tragic if understandable backlash has begun against Y2K warnings that is ultimately even more destructive: the claim that Y2K is a myth, a nonissue that will go away if the loud-mouths will just shut up. It will not. It is real. I believe Y2K will be the single biggest business crisis many of us will face in our life-times.... I've avoided writing a 'Y2K Fears' column until now be-cause I find it unseemly to be associated with the sky-is-falling types. I've been confident that American business, indeed global business, would address this problem early, aggressively, effectively. I was wrong. They didn't. We didn't."

—JIM SEYMOUR *of* **PC Magazine,** *February 10, 1998* #

Tom Atlee, who assembled the above references, is founder and co-director of the non-profit Co-Intelligence Institute and serves on the board of The Center for Group Learning. In 1991 he did community-building work in Belize and, funded by the German Marshall Fund, toured Czechoslovakia at the request of the Federal Environmental Ministry, introducing activists and government officials to ecologically sound, community-centered alternatives. In 1993 he organized an 8-month written dialogue on "societal intelligence" involving Robert Theobald, Fran Peavey, Howard Rheingold, Willis Harman, Hazel Henderson, Andrew Schmookler, Arnold Mindell, Duane Elgin, Charles Johnston, Eleanore M. Cooper and a dozen others. From 1989-1994 he edited and published *Thinkpeace,* a national journal of peacemaking strategy and philosophy. He served on the board of Berkeley's innovative Ecology Center and was a founding member of Bob Theobald's on-line Transformational Learning Community. For further information see www.co-intelligence.org

The Year 2000: Social Chaos or Social Transformation?

BY JOHN L. PETERSEN, MARGARET WHEATLEY, MYRON KELLNER-ROGERS

The millennial sun will first rise over human civilization in the independent republic of Kiribati, a group of some thirty low lying coral islands in the Pacific Ocean that straddle the equator and the International Date Line, halfway between Hawaii and Australia. This long-awaited sunrise marks the dawn of the year 2000, and quite possibly, the onset of unheralded disruptions in life as we know it in many parts of the globe. Kiribati's 81,000 Micronesians may observe nothing different about this dawn; they only received TV in 1989. However, for those who live in a world that relies on satellites, air, rail and ground transportation, manufacturing plants, electricity, heat, telephones, or TV, when the calendar clicks from '99 to '00, we will experience a true millennial shift. As the sun moves westward on January 1, 2000, as the date shifts silently within millions of computerized systems, we will begin to experience our computer-dependent world in an entirely new way. We will finally see the extent of the networked and interdependent processes we have created. At the stroke of midnight, the new millennium heralds the greatest challenge to modern society we have yet to face as a planetary community. Whether we experience this as chaos or social transformation will be influenced by what we do immediately.

We are describing the year 2000 problem, known as Y2K (K signifying 1000). Nicknamed at first "The Millennial Bug," increasing sensitivity to the magnitude of the impending crisis has escalated it to "The Millennial Bomb." The problem begins as a simple technical error. Large mainframe computers more than ten years old were not programmed to handle a four digit year. Sitting here now, on the threshold of the year 2000, it seems incomprehensible that computer programmers and microchip designers didn't plan for it. But when these billions of lines of computer code were being written, computer memory was very expensive. Remember when a computer only had 16 kilobytes of RAM? To save storage space, most programmers allocated only two digits to a year. 1993 is '93' in data files,

1917 is '17'. These two-digit dates exist on millions of files used as input to millions of applications. (The era in which this code was written was described by one programming veteran as "the Wild West." Programmers did whatever was required to get a product up and working; no one even thought about standards.)

The same thing happened in the production of microchips as recently as three years ago. Microprocessors and other integrated circuits are often just sophisticated calculators that count and do math. They count many things: fractions of seconds, days, inches, pounds, degrees, lumens, etc. Many chips that had a time function designed into them were only structured for this century. And when the date goes from '99 to '00 both they and the legacy software that has not been fixed will think it is still the 20th century — not 2000, but 1900.

Peter de Jager, who has been actively studying the problem and its implications since 1991, explains the computer math calculation: "I was born in 1955. If I ask the computer to calculate how old I am today, it subtracts 55 from 98 and announces that I'm 43. . . But what happens in the year 2000? The computer will subtract 55 from 00 and will state that I am minus 55 years old. This error will affect any calculation that produces or uses time spans. . . . If you want to sort by date, e.g., 1965, 1905, 1966, the resulting sequence would be 1905, 1965, 1966. However, if you add in a date record such as 2015, the computer, which reads only the last two digits of the date, sees 05, 15, 65, 66 and sorts them incorrectly. These are just two types of calculations that are going to produce garbage." [Peter de Jager, http://www.year2000.com].

The calculation problem explains why the computer system at Marks & Spencer department store in London recently destroyed tons of food during the process of doing a long-term forecast. The computer read 2002 as 1902. Instead of four more years of shelf life, the computer calculated that this food was ninety-six years old. It ordered it thrown out. [United Airlines, *Flight Talk Network,* February 1998]. A similar problem happened recently in the U.S. at the warehouse of a freeze-dried food manufacturer.

But Y2K is not about wasting good food. Date calculations affect millions more systems than those that deal with inventories, interest rates, or insurance policies. Every major aspect of our modern infrastructure has systems and equipment that rely on such calculations to perform their functions. We are dependent on computerized systems that contain date functions to effectively manage defense, transportation, power generation, manufacturing, telecommunications, finance, government, education, health care. The list is longer, but the picture is clear. We have created a world whose efficient functioning in all but the poorest and remotest areas is dependent on computers. It doesn't matter whether you personally use a computer, or that most people around the world don't even have telephones. The world's economic and political infrastructures rely on computers. And not isolated computers. We have created dense networks of reliance around the globe. We are networked together for economic and political purposes. Whatever happens in one part of the network has an impact on other parts of the network. We have created not only a computer-dependent society, but an interdependent planet.

We already have frequent experiences with how fragile these systems are, and how failure cascades through a networked system. While each of these systems relies on millions of lines of code that detail the required processing, they handle their routines in serial fashion. Any next step depends on the preceding step. This serial nature makes systems, no matter their size, vulnerable to even the slightest problem anywhere in the system. In 1990, ATT's long distance system experienced repeated failures. At that time, it took two million lines of computer code to keep the system operational. But these millions of lines of code were brought down by just three lines of faulty code.

And these systems are lean; redundancies are eliminated in the name of efficiency. This leanness also makes the system highly vulnerable. In May 1998, 90% of all pagers in the U.S. crashed for a day or longer because of the failure of one satellite. Late in 1997, the Internet could not deliver e-mail to the appropriate addresses because bad information from their one and only central source corrupted their servers.

Compounding the fragility of these systems is the fact that we can't see the extent of our interconnectedness. The networks that make modern life possible are masked by the technology. We only see the interdependencies when the relationships are disrupted — when a problem develops elsewhere and we notice that we too are having problems. When Asian markets failed last year, most U.S. businesses denied it would have much of an impact on our economy. Only recently have we felt the extent to which Asian economic woes affect us directly. Failure in one part of a system always exposes the levels of interconnectedness that otherwise go unnoticed — we suddenly see how our fates are linked together. We see how much we are participating with one another, sustaining one another.

Modern business is completely reliant on networks. Companies have vendors, suppliers, customers, outsourcers (all, of course, managed by computerized databases). For Y2K, these highly networked ways of doing business create a terrifying scenario. The networks mean that no one system can protect itself from Y2K failures by just attending to its own internal systems. General Motors, which has been working with extraordinary focus and diligence to bring their manufacturing plants up to Year 2000 compliance (based on their assessment that they were facing catastrophe) has 100,000 suppliers worldwide. Bringing their internal systems into compliance seems nearly impossible, but what then do they do with all those vendors who supply parts? GM experiences production stoppages whenever one key supplier goes on strike. What is the potential number of delays and shutdowns possible among 100,000 suppliers?

The nature of systems and our history with them paints a chilling picture of the Year 2000. We do not know the extent of the failures, or how we will be affected by them. But we do know with great certainty that as computers around the globe respond or fail when their calendars record 2000, we will see clearly the extent of our interdependence. We will see the ways in which we have woven the modern world together through our technology.

WHAT, ME WORRY?

Until quite recently, it's been difficult to interest most people in the Year 2000 problem. Those who are publicizing the problem (the World Wide Web is the source of the most extensive information on Y2K) exclaim about the general lack of awareness, or even the deliberate blindness that greets them. In our own investigation among many varieties of organizations and citizens, we've noted two general categories of response. In the first category, people acknowledge the problem but view it as restricted to a small number of businesses, or a limited number of consequences. People believe that Y2K affects only a few industries — primarily finance and insurance — seemingly because they deal with dates on policies and accounts. Others note that their organization is affected by Y2K, but still view it as a well-circumscribed issue that is being addressed by their information technology (IT) department. What's common to these comments is that people hold Y2K as a narrowly-focused, bounded problem. They seem oblivious to the networks in which they participate, or to the systems and interconnections of modern life.

The second category of reactions reveals the great collective faith in technology and science. People describe Y2K as a technical problem, and then enthusiastically state that human ingenuity and genius always find a way to solve these types of problems. Ecologist David Orr has noted that one of the fundamental beliefs of our time is that technology can be trusted to solve any problem it creates. If a software engineer goes on TV claiming to have created a program that can correct all systems, he is believed. After all, he's just what we've been expecting.

And then there is the uniqueness of the Year 2000 problem. At no other time in history have we been forced to deal with a deadline that is absolutely non-negotiable. In the past, we could always hope for a last-minute deal, or rely on round-the-clock bargaining, or pray for an eleventh hour savior. We have never had to stare into the future knowing the precise date when the crisis would materialize. In a bizarre fashion, the inevitability of this confrontation seems to add to people's denial of it. They know the date when the extent of the problem will surface, and choose not to worry about it until then.

However, this denial is quickly dissipating. Information on Y2K is expanding exponentially, matched by an escalation in adjectives used to describe it. More public figures are speaking out. This is critically important. With each calendar tick of this time, alternatives diminish and potential problems grow. We must develop strategies for preparing ourselves at all levels to deal with whatever Y2K presents to us with the millennium dawn.

What we know about Y2K: It is
- a technological problem that cannot be solved by technology
- the first-ever, non-negotiable deadline
- a systemic crisis that no one can solve alone
- a crisis that transcends boundaries and hierarchies
- an opportunity to evoke greater capacity from individuals and organizations
- an opportunity to simplify and redesign major systems

THE Y2K PROBLEM, REALLY

We'd like to describe in greater detail the extent of Y2K. As a global network of interrelated consequences, it begins at the center with the technical problem, legacy computer codes and embedded microchips. For the last thirty years thousands of programmers have been writing billions of lines of software code for the computers on which the world's economy and society now depend. Y2K reporter Ed Meagher describes "old, undocumented code written in over 2,500 different computer languages and executed on thousands of different hardware platforms being controlled by hundreds of different operating systems . . . [that generate] further complexity in the form of billions of six-character date fields stored in millions of databases that are used in calculations." ["The Complexity Factor" by Ed Meagher at http://www.year2000.com/archiveNFcomplexity.html].

The Gartner Group, a computer-industry research group, estimates that globally, 180 billion lines of software code will have to be screened, ["Industry Wakes Up to the Year 2000 Menace," *Fortune*, April 27, 1998]. Peter de Jager notes that it is not unusual for a company to have more than 100 million lines of code — the IRS, for instance, has at least 80 million lines. The Social Security Administration began working on its 30 million lines of code in 1991. After five years of work, in June 1996, 400 programmers had fixed only six million lines. The IRS has 88,000 programs on 80 mainframe computers to debug. By the end of last year they had cleaned up 2,000 programs. [*The Washington Post,* "If Computer Geeks Desert, IRS Codes Will Be Ciphers," December 24, 1997].

Capers Jones, head of Software Productivity Research, a firm that tracks programmer productivity, estimates that finding, fixing and testing all Y2K-affected software would require over 700,000 person-years. [*Business Week,* March 2, 1998]. Programmers have been brought out of retirement and are receiving extraordinary wages and benefits to stick with this problem, but we are out of time. There aren't nearly enough programmers nor hours remaining before January 1, 2000.

Also at the center of this technical time bomb are the embedded microprocessors. There are somewhat over a billion of these hardware chips located in systems worldwide. They sustain the world's manufacturing and engineering base. They exist in traffic lights, elevators, water, gas, and electricity control systems. They're in medical equipment and military and navigation systems. America's air traffic control system is dependent upon them. They're located in the track beds of railroad systems and in the satellites that circle the earth. Global telecommunications are heavily dependent on them. Modern cars contain about two dozen microprocessors. The average American comes in contact with 70 microprocessors before noon every day. Many of these chips aren't date sensitive, but a great number are, and engineers looking at long-ago-installed systems don't know for sure which is which. To complicate things further, not all chips behave the same. Recent tests have shown that two chips of the same model installed in two different computers but performing the same function are not equally sensitive to the year-end problem. One shuts down and the other doesn't.

It is impossible to locate all of these chips in the remaining months, nor can we replace all those that are identified. Those more than three years old are obsolete and are probably not available in the marketplace. The solution in those cases is to redesign and remanufacture that part of the system — which often makes starting over with new equipment the best option. That is why some companies are junking their computer systems and spending millions, even hundreds of millions, to replace everything. It at least ensures that their internal systems work.

At issue is time, people, money, and the nature of systems. These technical problems are exacerbated by government and business leaders who haven't yet fully understood the potential significance of this issue for their own organizations, to say nothing of the greater economic implications. The U.S. leads all other developed nations in addressing this issue, minimally by six to nine months. Yet in a recent survey of American corporate chief information officers, 70% of them expressed the belief that even their companies would not be completely prepared for Y2K. Additionally, 50% of them acknowledged that they would not fly during January 2000. If America is the global leader in Y2K efforts, these CIO comments are indeed sobering.

The economic impacts for the global economy are enormous and unknown. The Gartner Group projects that the total cost of dealing with Y2K worldwide will be somewhere between $300 billion to $600 billion — and these are only direct costs associated with trying to remedy the problem. (These estimates keep rising every quarter now.) The Office of Management and Budget (OMB), in a recently released Quarterly Report, estimated total government Y2K expense at $3.9 billion. This figure was based only on federal agency estimates; the OMB warned that this estimate might be as much as 90% too low considering the increasing labor shortage and expected growing remediation costs as January 1, 2000 looms nearer. And in June of this year, it was announced that federal agencies had already spent five billion dollars. Of twenty-four agencies, fifteen reported being behind schedule.

These numbers don't consider the loss of output caused by diverting resources to forestall this crisis. In more and more businesses, expenditures for R&D and modernization are being diverted to Y2K budgets. *Business Week* in March 1998 estimated that the Year 2000 economic damage alone would be $119 billion. When potential lawsuits and secondary effects are added to this—people suing over everything from stalled elevators to malfunctioning nuclear power plants—the cost easily could be over $1 trillion.

But these problems and estimates don't begin to account for the potential impact of Y2K. The larger significance of this bomb becomes apparent when we consider the next circle of the global network—the organizational relationships that technology makes possible.

WHO WORKS WITH WHOM?

The global economy is dependent upon computers both directly and indirectly. Whether it's your PC at home, the workstation on a local area network, or the GPS or mobile telephone that you carry, all are integral parts of larger networks where computers are directly connected together. As we've learned, failure in a single component can crash the whole system; that system could be an automobile, a train, an aircraft, an electric power plant, a bank, a government agency, a stock exchange, an international telephone system, the air traffic control system. If every possible date-sensitive hardware and software bug hasn't been fixed in a larger system, just one programming glitch or one isolated chip potentially can bring down the whole thing.

While there isn't enough time or technical people to solve the Y2K problem before the end of next year, we might hope that critical aspects of our infrastructure are tackling this problem with extreme diligence. But this isn't true. America's electric power industry is in danger of massive failures, as described in *Business Week's* February '98 cover story on Y2K. They report that "electric utilities are only now becoming aware that programmable controllers — which have replaced mechanical relays in virtually all electricity-generating plants and control rooms — may behave badly or even freeze up when 2000 arrives. Many utilities are just getting a handle on the problem." It's not only nuclear power plants that are the source of concern, although problems there are scary enough. In one Year 2000 test, notes Jared S.Wermiel, leader of the Y2K effort at the Nuclear Regulatory Commission, the security computer at a nuclear power plant failed by opening vital areas that are normally locked. Given the complexity and the need to test, "it wouldn't surprise me if certain plants find that they are not Year 2000-ready and have to shut down." [http://www.igs.net/~tonyc/y2kbusweek.html].

Other electric utility analysts paint a bleaker picture. Rick Cowles, who reports on the electric utility industry, said at the end of February: "Not one electric company [that he had talked to] has started a serious remediation effort on its embedded controls. Not one. Yes, there's been some testing going on, and a few pilot projects here and there, but for the most part it is still business-as-usual, as if there

"The [electric utility] industry is fiddling whilst the infrastructure burns."

—RICK COWLES

were 97 months to go, not 97 weeks. ["Industry Gridlock," Rick Cowles, February 27, 1998, http://www.y2ktimebomb.com/PP/RC/rc9808.htm]. After attending one industry trade show, Cowles stated that, "Based on what I learned at DistribuTECH '98, I am convinced there is a 100% chance that a major portion of the domestic electrical infrastructure will be lost as a result of the Year 2000 computer and embedded systems problem. The industry is fiddling whilst the infrastructure burns." [Cowles, January 23, 1998, ibid].

The Federal Aviation Administration is also very vulnerable but quite optimistic. "We're on one hand working to get those computers Year 2000 compliant, but at the same time we're working on replacing those computers," said Paul Takemoto, a spokesman for the FAA in early '98. At the twenty Air Route Traffic Control Centers, there is a host computer and a backup system. All forty of these machines — mid-'80s vintage IBM 3083 mainframes — are affected. And then there are the satellites with embedded chips, individual systems in each airplane, and air traffic control systems around the globe. Lufthansa already has announced it will not fly its aircraft during the first days of 2000.

WHO ELSE IS AFFECTED?

But the interdependency problem extends far beyond single businesses, or even entire industries. Indirect relationships extend like tentacles into many other networks, creating the potential for massive disruptions of service.

Let's hope that your work organization spends a great deal of money and time to get its entire information system compliant. You know yours is going to function. But on the second of January 2000 the phone calls start. It's your banker. "There's been a problem," he says. They've lost access to your account information and until they solve the problem and get the backup loaded on the new system, they are unable to process your payroll. "We don't have any idea how long it will take," the president says.

Then someone tells you that on the news there's a story that the whole IRS is down and that they can neither accept nor process tax information. Social Security, Federal Housing, Welfare — none of these agencies are capable of issuing checks for the foreseeable future. Major airlines aren't flying, waiting to see if there is still integrity in the air traffic control system. And manufacturing across the country is screeching to a halt because of failures in their supply chain. (After years of developing just-in-time systems, there is no inventory on hand — suppliers have been required to deliver parts as needed. There is no slack in these systems to tolerate even minor delivery problems.) Ground and rail transport have been disrupted, and food shortages appear within three to six days in major metropolises. Hospitals, dealing with the failure of medical equipment, and the loss of shipments of medicine, are forced to deny non-essential treatment, and in some cases are providing essential care in pre-technical ways.

It's a rolling wave of interdependent failures. And it reaches across the country and the world to touch people who, in most cases, didn't know they were linked to others. Depending on what systems fail, very few but strategically placed failures would initiate a major economic cascade. Just problems with power companies and phone systems alone would cause real havoc. (In spring 1998, a problem in ATT rendered all credit card machines useless for a day. How much revenue was lost by businesses?) If only twenty percent of businesses and government agencies crash at the same time, major failures would ensue.

In an interdependent system, solving most of the problems is no solution. As Y2K reporter Ed Meagher describes:

"It is not enough to solve simply 'most of these problems.' The integration of these systems requires that we solve virtually all of them. Our ability as an economy and as a society to deal with disruptions and breakdowns in our critical systems is minuscule. Our worst case scenarios have never envisioned multiple, parallel systemic failures. Just in time inventory has led to just in time provisioning. Costs have been squeezed out of all of our critical infrastructure systems repeatedly over time based on the ubiquity and reliability of these integrated systems. The human factor, found costly, slow, and less reliable has been purged over time from our systems. Single, simple failures can be dealt with; complex, multiple failures have been considered too remote a possibility and therefore too expensive to plan for." [The Complexity Factor, Ed Meagher].

The city of New York began to understand this last September. The governor of New York State banned all nonessential IT projects to minimize the disruption caused by the year 2000 bomb after reading a detailed report that forecasts the millennium will throw New

York City into chaos, with power supplies, schools, hospitals, transport, and the finance sector likely to suffer severe disruption. Compounding the city's Y2K risks is the recent departure of the head of its Year 2000 project to a job in the private sector. [http://www.computerweekly.co. uk/news/ll_9_97].

But of course the anticipated problems extend far beyond U.S. shores. In February 1998, the *Bangkok Post* reported that Phillip Dodd, a Unysis Y2K expert, expects that upward of 70% of the businesses in Asia will fail outright or experience severe hardship because of Y2K. The Central Intelligence Agency supports this with their own analysis: "We're concerned about the potential disruption of power grids, telecommunications and banking services, among other possible fallout, especially in countries already torn by political tensions." [Reuters: "CIA: Year 2000 to hit basic services: Agency warns that many nations aren't ready for disruption," Jim Wolf, May 7, 1998].

A growing number of assessments of this kind have led Dr. Edward Yardeni, the chief economist of Deutsche Morgan Grenfell, to keep raising the probability of a deep global recession in 2000-2001 as the result of Y2K. His present estimate of the potential for such a recession now hovers at about 70%, up from 40% at the end of 1997. [http://www.Yardeni.com].

HOW MIGHT WE RESPOND?

As individuals, nations, and as a global society, do we have a choice as to how we might respond to Y2K, however problems materialize? The question of alternative social responses lies at the outer edges of the interlocking circles of technology and system relationships. At present, potential societal reactions receive almost no attention. But we firmly believe that it is the central most important place to focus public attention and individual ingenuity. Y2K is a technology-induced problem, but it will not and cannot be solved by technology. It creates societal problems that can only be solved by humans. We must begin to address potential social responses. We need to be engaged in this discourse within our organizations, our communities, and across the traditional boundaries of competition and national borders. Without such planning, we will slide into the Year 2000 as hapless victims of our technology.

Even where there is some recognition of the potential disruptions or chaos that Y2K might create, there's a powerful dynamic of secrecy preventing us from engaging in these conversations. Leaders don't want to panic their citizens. Employees don't want to panic their bosses. Corporations don't want to panic investors. Lawyers don't want their clients to confess to anything. But as psychotherapist and information systems consultant Dr. Douglass Carmichael (see his article on page 60) has written:

"Those who want to hush the problem ('Don't talk about it, people will panic' and 'We don't know for sure') are having three effects. First, they are preventing a more rigorous investigation of the extent of the problem. Second, they are slowing down the awareness of the intensity of the problem as currently understood and the urgency of the need for solutions, given the current assessment of the risks. Third, they are making almost certain a higher degree of ultimate panic, in anger, under conditions of shock." [http://www.tmn.com/~doug].

Haven't we yet learned the consequences of secrecy? When people are kept in the dark, or fed misleading information, their confidence in leaders quickly erodes. In the absence of real information, people fill the information vacuum with rumors and fear. And whenever we feel excluded, we have no choice but to withdraw and focus on self-protective measures. As the veil of secrecy thickens, the capacity for public discourse and shared participation in solution-finding disappears. People no longer believe anything or anybody — we become unavailable, distrusting and focused only on self-preservation. Our history with the problems created by secrecy has led CEO Norman Augustine to advise leaders in crisis to: "Tell the truth and tell it fast." ["Managing the Crisis You Tried to Prevent," *Harvard Business Review,* Nov-Dec. 1995, 158].

Behaviors induced by secrecy are not the only human responses available. Time and again we observe a much more positive human response during times of crisis. When an earthquake strikes, or a bomb goes off, or a flood or fire destroys a community, people respond with astonishing capacity and effectiveness. They use any available materials to save and rescue, they perform acts of pure altruism, they open their homes to one another, they finally learn who their neighbors are. We've interviewed many people who participated in the aftermath of a disaster, and as they report on their experiences, it is clear that their participation changed their lives. They discovered new capacities in themselves and in their communities. They exceeded all expectations. They were surrounded by feats of caring and courage. They contributed to getting systems restored with a speed that defied all estimates.

When chaos strikes, there's simply no time for secrecy; leaders have no choice but to engage every willing soul. And the field for improvisation is wide open — no emergency preparedness drill ever prepares people for what they actually end up doing. Individual initiative and involvement are essential. Yet surprisingly, in the midst of conditions of devastation and fear, people report how good they feel about themselves and their colleagues. These crisis experiences are memorable because the best of us becomes visible and available. We've observed this in America, and in Bangladesh, where the poorest of the poor responded to the needs of their most destitute neighbors rather than accepting relief for themselves.

What we know about people in crisis:
- shared purpose and meaning brings people together
- people display unparalleled levels of creativity and resourcefulness
- people want to help others—individual agendas fade immediately
- people learn instantly and respond at lightning speed
- the more information people get, the smarter their responses
- leadership behaviors (not roles) appear everywhere, as needed
- people experiment constantly to find what works

WHO MIGHT WE BECOME?

As we sit staring into the unknown dimensions of a global crisis whose timing is non-negotiable, what responses are available to us as a human community? An effective way to explore this question is to develop potential scenarios of possible social behaviors. Scenario planning is an increasingly accepted technique for identifying the spectrum of possible futures that are most important to an organization or society. In selecting among many possible futures, it is most useful to look at those that account for the greatest uncertainty and the greatest impact.

For Y2K, David Isenberg (a former AT&T telecommunications expert, now at Isen.Com) has identified the two variables which seem obvious — the range of technical failures from isolated to multiple, and the potential social responses, from chaos to coherence.* Both variables are critical and uncertain and are arrayed as a pair of crossing axes. When displayed in this way, four different general futures emerge.

(1) In the upper left quadrant, if technical failures are isolated and society doesn't respond to those failures, nothing of significance will happen. Isenberg labels this the "Official Future" because it reflects present behavior on the part of leaders and organizations.

(2) The upper right quadrant describes a time where technical failures are still isolated, but the public responds to these with panic,

perhaps fanned by the media or by stonewalling leaders. Termed "A Whiff of Smoke," the situation is analogous to the panic caused in a theater by someone who smells smoke and spreads an alarm, even though it is discovered that there is no fire. This world could evolve from a press report that fans the flames of panic over what starts as a minor credit card glitch (for example) and, fueled by rumors, turns nothing into a major social problem with runs on banks, etc. The lower quadrants describe far more negative scenarios.

(3) The lower right, "Millennial Apocalypse" presumes large-scale technical failure coupled with social breakdown as the organizational, political and economic systems come apart.

(4) The lower left quadrant, "Human Spirit," posits a society that, in the face of clear adversity, calls on each of us to collaborate in solving the problems of breakdown.

SINCE ESSENTIALLY we are out of time and resources for preventing widespread Y2K failures, a growing number of observers believe that the only plausible future scenarios worth contemplating are those in the lower half of the matrix (scenarios 3 and 4). The major question before us is how will society respond to what is almost certain to be widespread and cascading technological failures?

Here is one possible natural evolution of the problem: early, perhaps even in '98, the press could start something bad long before it was clear how serious the problem was and how society would react to it. There could be an interim scenario where a serious technical problem turned into a major social problem from lack of adaquate positive social response. This "Small Theatre Fire" future could be the kind of situation where people overreact and trample themselves trying to get to the exits from a small fire that is routinely extinguished.

If the technical situation is bad, a somewhat more ominous situation could evolve where government, exerting no clear positive leadership and seeing no alternative to chaos, cracks down so as not to lose control. A common historical response to social chaos has been for the government to intervene in a non-democratic, sometimes brutal fashion. In response to Y2K, "techno-fascism" is a plausible scenario: governments and large corporations would intervene to try to contain the damage, rather than build for the future. This dictatorial approach would be accompanied by secrecy about the real extent of the problem and ultimately fueled by the cries of distress, prior to 2000, from a society that has realized its major systems are about to fail and that it is too late to do anything about it.

COLLABORATION IS OUR ONLY CHOICE

Obviously, the scenario worth working towards is "Human Spirit," a world where the best of human creativity is enabled and the highest common good becomes the objective. In this world we all work together, developing a very broad, powerful, synergistic, self-organizing force focused on determining what humanity should be doing in the next 18 months to plan for the aftermath of the down stroke of Y2K. This requires that we understand Y2K not as a technical problem, but as a systemic, worldwide event that can only be resolved by new social relationships. All of us need to become very wise and very engaged very fast and develop entirely new processes for working together. Systems issues cannot be resolved by hiding behind traditional boundaries or by clinging to competitive strategies. Systems require collaboration and the dissolution of existing boundaries. Our only hope for healthy responses to Y2K-induced failures is to participate together in new collaborative relationships.

At present, individuals and organizations are being encouraged to protect themselves, to focus on solving "their" problem. In a systems' world, this is insane. The problems are not isolated, therefore no isolated responses will work. The longer we pursue strategies for individual survival, the less time we have to create any viable, systemic solutions. None of the boundaries we've created across industries, organizations, communities, or nation states give us any protection in the face of Y2K. We must stop the messages of fragmentation now and focus resources and leadership on figuring out how to engage everyone, at all levels, in all systems.

As threatening as Y2K is, it also gives us the unparalleled opportunity to figure out new and simplified ways of working together. GM's chief information officer, Ralph Szygenda, has said that Y2K is the cruelest trick ever played on us by technology, but that it also represents a great opportunity for change. [*Fortune*, April 27, 1998]. It demands that we let go of traditional boundaries and roles in the pursuit of new, streamlined systems, ones that are less complex than the entangled ones that have evolved over the past thirty years.

There's an interesting lesson here about involvement that comes from the Oklahoma City bombing in 1995. Just a few weeks prior the bombing, agencies from all over the city conducted an emergency preparedness drill as part of normal civil defense practice. They did not prepare themselves for a bomb blast, but they did work together on other disaster scenarios. The most significant accomplishment of the drill was to create an invisible infrastructure of trusting relationships. When the bomb went off, that infrastructure displayed itself as an essential resource—people could work together easily, even in the face of horror. Many lives were saved and systems were restored at an unprecedented rate because people from all over the community worked together so well.

But there's more to this story. One significant player had been excluded from the preparedness drill, and that was the FBI. No one thought they'd ever be involved in a federal matter. To this day, people in Oklahoma City speak resentfully of the manner in which the FBI came in, pushed them aside, and offered no explanations for their behavior. In the absence of trusting relationships, some form of techno-fascism is the only recourse. Elizabeth Dole, as president of the American Red Cross, commented: "The midst of a disaster is the poorest possible time to establish new relationships and to introduce ourselves to new organizations . . . . When you have taken the time to build rapport, then you can make a call at 2 a.m. when the river's rising and expect to launch a well-planned, smoothly conducted response." [quoted in "Managing the Crisis You Tried to Prevent," Norman Augustine, *Harvard Business Review,* Nov-Dec 1995, 151].

The scenario of communities and organizations working together in new ways demands a very different and immediate response not only from leaders but from each of us. We'd like to describe a number of actions that need to begin immediately.

WHAT LEADERS MUST DO

We urge leaders to give up trying to carry this burden alone, or trying to reestablish a world that is irretrievably broken. We need leaders to be catalysts for the emergence of a new world. They cannot lead us through this in traditional ways. No leader or senior team can determine what needs to be done. No single group can assess the complexity of these systems and where the consequences of failure might be felt. The unknown but complex implications of Y2K demand that leaders support unparalleled levels of participation — more broad-based and inclusive than ever imagined. If we are to go through this crisis together rather than bunkered down and focused only on individual security, leaders must begin right now to convene us. The first work of leaders then, is to create the resources for groups to come together in conversations that will reveal the interconnections. Boundaries need to dissolve. Hierarchies are irrelevant. Courageous leaders will understand that they must surrender the illusion of control and seek solutions from the great networks and communities within their domain. They must move past the dynamics of competi-

*At present, individuals and organizations
are being encouraged to protect themselves,
to focus on solving "their" problem.
In a systems' world, this is insane.*

tion and support us in developing society-wide solutions.

Leaders can encourage us to seek out those we have excluded and insist that they be invited in to all deliberations. Leaders can provide the time and resources for people to assess what is critical for the organization or community to sustain — its mission, its functions, its relationships, its unique qualities. From these conversations and plans, we will learn to know one another and to know what we value. In sudden crises, people instantly share a sense of meaning and purpose. For Y2K, we have at least a little lead time to develop a cohesive sense of what might happen and how we hope to respond.

Secrecy must be replaced by full and frequent disclosure of information. The only way to prevent driving people into isolated and self-preserving behaviors is to entrust us with difficult, even fearsome information, and then to insist that we work together.

No leader anywhere can ignore these needs or delay their implementation.

WHAT COMMUNITIES MUST DO

Communities need to assess where they are most vulnerable and develop contingency plans. Such assessment and planning needs to occur not just within individual locales but also in geographic regions. These activities can be initiated by existing community networks—for example, civic organizations such as Lions or Rotary, Council of Churches, Chamber of Commerce, the United Way. But new and expansive alliances are required, so planning activities need quickly to extend beyond traditional borders. We envision residents of all ages and experience coming together to do these audits and planning. Within each community and region, assessments and contingency plans need to be in place for disruptions or loss of service for:

- all utilities — electricity, water, gas, phones
- food supplies
- public safety
- health care

- government payments to individuals and organizations
- residents most at risk, e.g. the elderly and those requiring medications

WHAT ORGANIZATIONS MUST DO

Organizations need to move Y2K from the domain of technology experts into the entire organization. Everyone in the organization has something important to contribute to this work. Assessment and contingency plans need to focus on:

- how the organization will perform essential tasks in the absence of present systems
- how the organization will respond to failures or slowdowns in information and supplies
- what simplified systems can be developed now to replace existing ones
- relationships with suppliers, customers, clients, communities — how we will work together
- developing systems to ensure open and full access to information

The trust and loyalty developed through these strategic conversations and joint planning will pay enormous dividends later on, even if projected breakdowns don't materialize. Corporate and community experience with scenario planning has taught an important principle: we don't need to be able to predict the future in order to be well-prepared for it. In developing scenarios, information is sought from all over. People think together about its implications and thus become smarter as individuals and as teams. Whatever future then materializes is dealt with by people who are more intelligent and who know how to work well together.

And such planning needs to occur at the level of entire industries. Strained relationships engendered by competitive pressures need to be put aside so that people can collaboratively search for ways to sustain the very fabric of their industry. How will power grids be maintained nationally? Or national systems of food transport? How will supply chains for manufacturing in any industry be sustained?

WHAT YOU CAN DO

We urge you to get involved in Y2K, wherever you are, and in whatever organizations you participate. We can't leave this issue to others to solve for us, nor can we wait for anyone else to assert leadership. You can begin to ask questions; you can begin to convene groups of interested friends and colleagues; you can engage local and business leaders; you can educate yourself and others (start with http://www.Year2000.com and http://www.Y2K.com for up-to-date information and resources). This is our problem. And as an African proverb reminds us, if you think you're too small to make a difference, try going to bed with a mosquito in the room.

THE CRISIS IS NOW

There is no time left to waste. Every week decreases our options. At the mid-May meeting of leaders from the G8, a communique was issued that expressed their shared sensitivity to the "vast implications" of Y2K, particularly in "defense, transport, telecommunications, financial services, energy, and environmental sectors," and the interdependencies among these sectors. (Strangely, their list excludes from concern government systems, manufacturing and distribution systems.) They vowed to "take further urgent action" and to work with one another, and relevant organizations and agencies. But no budget was established, and no specific activities were announced. Such behavior — the issuing of a communique, the promises of collaboration and further investigation — are all too common in our late 20th century political landscape.

But the earth continues to circle the sun, and the calendar relentlessly progresses toward the Year 2000. If we cannot immediately change from rhetoric to action, from politics to participation, if we do not immediately turn to one another and work together for the common good, we will stand fearfully in that new dawn and suffer consequences that might well have been avoided if we had learned to stand together now. #

Copyright © 1998 by John L. Petersen, Margaret Wheatley, Myron Kellner-Rogers. Reprinted with permission of the authors.

*See "Scenarios Facing Year 2000" by David S. Isenberg on http://www.isen.com/archives/980515.html

John L. Petersen is president of The Arlington Institute, a Washington DC area research institute. He is a futurist who specializes in thinking about the long range security implications of global change. He is author of the award-winning book, *The Road to 2015: Profiles of the Future* and his latest book is *Out of the Blue - Wild Cards and Other Big Future Surprises,* which deals with potential events such as Y2K. He can be reached at 703-243-7070 or johnp@arlinst.org.
Margaret Wheatley and **Myron Kellner-Rogers** are authors and consultants to business. *A Simpler Way,* their book on organizational de-

sign, was published in 1997. Dr. Wheatley's previous book, *Leadership & the New Science,* was recently named one of the 10 best management books ever, and it also was voted best management book in 1992 in *Industry Week,* and again in 1995 by a syndicated management columnist. Their consulting work takes them these days to Brazil, Mexico, South Africa, Australasia and Europe. In the States, they've worked with a very wide array of organizations.

How to Think About Y2K

*For those who realize it is going to be a pretty big deal
and who've always wanted a better world*

BY TOM ATLEE

The first things you probably noticed about Y2K were:
a) It is unbelievably stupid.
b) It is unbelievably scary.

I mean, think about it for a minute: How could a bunch of geeks pull the rug out from under the most powerful civilization in the history of the planet—and do it by accident, no less?! And how could such a bizarre catastrophe of potentially mind-boggling proportions be happening in the middle of your otherwise full and frustrating life, when you can't even find a few spare moments to think clearly about it?! It isn't fair!

I feel thoroughly confident in observing that this is not the life you signed up for.

But while you're doing the rumba with your overwhelm and denial, don't overlook the most obvious and powerful secret about Y2K: It is going to seriously mess up business-as-usual. If you look closely at this fact, you may notice a very big blessing inside that monstrous curse—some intense gilding around that thunder-pumping storm cloud.

Think about it:

Business-as-usual has two functions:
a) To keep most of us relatively comfortable and functioning
and
b) To keep The Establishment established.

When business-as-usual is messed with, both us and The Establishement get messed with. To the extent business-as-usual comes apart because of Y2K, most of us are going to find ourselves notoriously uncomfortable and non-functional. And The Establishment is going to find itself pretty thoroughly disestablished. We're going to end up with a lot of seriously unhappy people immersed in a playful little vortex of chaos. It's enough to make Antidisestablishmentarianists out of all of us.

So how do we think about this?

As we contemplate the seriousness of our plight, most of us have one of two reactions:

a) I don't like this one bit: I want to go home now.

b) I don't like this two bits: I want to wake up.

Unfortunately, we're already home and this isn't a dream. We're kind of stuck here.

As water was flooding the Titanic's engine room, a passenger told the ship's designer, "But the Titanic cannot sink." The designer replied, emphatically: "It *can*. And it *will*."

Realizing, at last, that we're not going to be able to get up and leave the theater, we resolve to get practical. In a moment of clarity, we say to ourselves:

a) I'm heading for the hills!!

b) What will become of my mother/ job/ dream house/ career/ cat/ and everything else precious to me...?!!

Well, since everyone else that runs into this particular wall (Y2K) has exactly the same thoughts, we can rest assured that the hills are going to be filled with all those folks we're trying to get away from. The first wave will be the rich folks who will drive up the rural real estate prices. The next wave will be the stragglers like most of the rest of us who will make all those country farmers edgy and over-whelm the capacity of small towns and forests to support the incoming crush of humanity. The final wave will be the hungry marauders, arriving to gather up all the resources that drained out of the cities months before.

"Shit," we think. "That's not going to work very well."

Same for our mothers and cats and hopes for a golden retirement. They're all in the same soup with the rest of us. I mean, this is a pretty big wave. Lots is going to get washed away.

I'd like to take this opportunity to suggest that all this "How To Save Yourself and Your Loved Ones and Prosper at the End of the World" is just real old-fashioned thinking. It obviously won't get us very far. I'd like to suggest that it is time for something new. It is time to Think Big.

The new question—the Big Question—is "What Does It Mean To Be A Human Being Alive At This Enormous Moment In History?"

This isn't a time for figuring out how much you can stuff into your backpack before the thousand-mile hike (you won't be able to carry it all, anyway).

This is a time for figuring out how to change the rudder of civilization. This is a once-in-a-millennium opportunity.

Everything is coming apart. What shape is it going to come together in? That is the question we'll be answering with our lives. This is a time to imagine your great grandchildren looking back and saying: "Wow! My Granddaddy/ Grandmommy was alive then, and they were part of making that incredible stuff happen!!"

This is like the American Revolution—but much, much more so. We have the fate of humanity in our hands, for real this time. What happens in the next few years will make all the difference in the world, I assure you. Don't twiddle it away trying to figure out how to hide until the storm's over. The storm may not be over for some time. And if it gets you, wouldn't you rather have died making a difference instead of crouched in a tiny corner of the background scenery?

Think about it.

Go ahead. Take a break and think about it.

(But of course, you're not going to do that. You're going to continue reading. I always do...)

One needs to think not only about survival,
but survival of what.
—MARY CATHERINE BATESON

So now let's talk about what's really worth living for.

A sustainable, just world made up of resilient, vibrant communities.

That's not what we have now, and it's not what we're going to have in the Year 2000, no matter what happens. But in the Year 2000 a lot of what keeps us from realizing that vision is probably going to come undone. We won't have to *take* it apart. It will just stop working. At that point we'll have a chance to turn the rudder of our civilization—or at least *try* to do so—so that when the motors start up again, the ship is headed in a different direction—towards a sustainable, just world made up of resilient, vibrant communities.

I'm choosing my metaphors carefully here. This isn't something we're going to *build* and then *have*. This is a turning of the rudder, a changing of direction.

What can we do so that, the further into the future our civilization goes, the more it becomes a sustainable, just world made up of resilient, vibrant communties? That's what we have a chance to influence—in a big, ugly, one-time-only, going-out-of-business-sale way.

BUT FIRST OFF, we need to face two Y2K realities:

a) Most people are going to be trying to survive. They're not going to be trying to change the world. The world will be changing fast enough around them, thank you, without any effort on their part.

b) Total collapse will favor negative directions rather than positive ones. If things get bad enough, we're all going to end up in gangland, with local warlords doling out the goods to their loyal followers, everyone else being food. (cf. Douglass Carmichael's scenarios.)

These two realities suggest a pretty clear strategy: We will use community survival preparations as the carrier wave for the change in direction that we want to see.

Here are some examples of how that might play out (see also *Protecting Our Community from Computer Chaos* by Paul Glover, page 112):

• When people move out of the cities—instead of doing an individual survivalist trip, they could move into experimental ecovillages. The more such villages there are, the richer the possibilities will be when the Y2K dust settles. (Of course, those ecovillages need to be in collaborative, mutually supporting relationships with the communities around them, or they, too, will become almost as vulnerable as lone survivalists.)

• People staying put can be shown how their survival depends on how well they know and work with their neighbors. Suddenly we may find it much easier to get people out to community events, fairs, work projects, parties, etc. We can do open space conferences and study circles on gathering rainwater, generating solar power, doing conflict resolution, decision-making, organic gardening, and bike repair. Sustainable technology marketeers and salespeople should have a field day preparing folks for off-the-grid living. (Take note, you socially-conscious investors!)

• There is *lots* to do together to help prepare a community for Y2K. Public officials need to be educated, pressured and inspired. Local businesses need to be awakened to the problem and helped towards Y2K-readiness. Agencies in charge of water, sewage, security, and other necessary services need to be pushed into wise, effective action. Emergency services need to be expanded to support much larger populations than they have envisioned in the past. Schools, churches, businesses, nonprofits and other organizations need to be engaged in a community-wide effort. Everyone has something to contribute, and everyone will be a beneficiary. (History shows that, even when communities have prepared in inappropriate ways for what eventually happens, the very act of preparing together has created a collective resilience that enables them to cope successfully with the unexpected crisis.)

• Since mass participation is a necessity in this effort—and since American populations are ill prepared to either collaborate or to blindly follow orders—this is a fantastic opportunity to experiment with new forms of collective decision-making, collective reflection and learning, and self-organized activity. There are hundreds of approaches to this (see my co-intelligence website for the tip of the iceberg), and all the practitioners of these leading-edge approaches can set aside their proprietary interests and dive into the fray getting the public addicted to the co-creation of their communal future.

• Local, ecological, and cooperative economic forms can be promoted because the economic infrastructure may no longer exist for the kind of massive export-import commerce and waste removal we're used to. Without that mega-economic infrastructure, we're left with neighbors working together to create what they need out of local resources—or else stealing from each other. Community livelihood may not come from anywhere else—for weeks or months—or even years.

• Racial and economic justice can be advanced through the realization that unfairness and hatred can blow apart communities just when they most need mutual aid to survive, when the business-as-usual systems of support and control are removed. If the cops can't come, where will social order come from? It's you and me and our ability to hear each other and act together as peers for our mutual benefit, for real.

• Existing county and bioregional networking will need to be expanded because no community can plot its course alone through times of breakdown. Any individual, group or community that is unduly advantaged will become a target; and possessiveness about resources will undermine everyone's ability to make this work. Creative sharing and making do, by everyone, at all levels of social organization, is the only thing that will sustain social cohesion in the likely hard times ahead.

• Companies trying to prepare for the new era can invest in eco-efficiency and local operations which make them less vulnerable to infrastructure breakdowns. While planning for Year 2000 contingencies, wise companies will look beyond 2000 to 2010 and 2020, and use the demands of Y2K to become more resilient in many ways to better face all the challenges of the new century. They'll find they need to collaborate much more with their suppliers, customers and even competitors, in order to make it through. In addition, community activists may find companies more responsive to community concerns, even such radical ideas as local currency and barter systems, when their survival is on the line. Programs like the Natural Step and industrial ecology could make good use of the demands of this new era.

• National governments have a chance to empower communities—or at least to "download" federal functions, like they've been trying to do for years. (We may not like this trend, but you have to admit, it could serve democratic decentralization, if we play our cards right.) Communities should pressure national governments to early-on identify and ensure a safety net of the minimal vital infrastructure needed to supply basic food, water, heat, security, etc., to community-based populations. The Y2K-readiness of these safety-net infrastructures must take precedence over all other Y2K-readiness projects. Politicians and governments need to get this message soon. (This is to prevent the worst possible collapses.) Communities also need to speak out against undue use of police and military force as a strategy for keeping social order in high-stress times; if state power gets out of hand, we may slide into fascism, which will make it all that much harder to turn the rudder. (Some people suggest that the collapse of the infrastructure would make fascistic centralization impossible, but we shouldn't underestimate the creativity of fascists.) Of course, minimizing the need for state power requires a high level of responsibility by communities, themselves, to keep order. (Civilian-based defense is a resource for this.)

• Similar community-based preparations should be encouraged internationally from both the governmental and grassroots levels. With the potential for the spread of toxic and nuclear substances (released by Y2K-caused accidents), diseases (caused by Y2K-damaged public hygiene infrastructure), migrating populations and social unrest (caused by Y2K-stimulated deprivation), we have no choice but to work for resilient, just communities in as many places as possible. We're definitely into an era of one-worldism, like it or not. We might as well make it a desirable one world.

• At a deeply personal level, the demands of Y2K will stretch many of us to—and beyond—our limits. Even now, there are dramatic opportunities for personal, psychological and spiritual growth—and for mutual support and service. We are facing a threat of death and loss unprecedented in the lives of most Americans and millions of others. Let us pray we emerge from Y2K wiser and more mature than when we went into it.

• Artists, performers, storytellers, filmmakers, documentarians, journalists and all the other media web-weavers (both mass and local) can help us cope, adapt and mature through the challenges of this era. They can provide models, ideals, insights, life-narratives and emotional perspective to deepen our experience. When they do, they will be creating a culture of sustainability, fairness, cooperation and meaning right before our eyes. I expect it will be difficult to get that new-culture genie back into the bottle, once it's out. A new culture is a new culture.

How far can we get in any of these realms? That depends to a great extent on how quickly we wake up to the unbelievable opportunity we have. Right now it is falling out of the sky into our laps. The universe is saying to us: "You want a revolution? You want transformation? You want a new world? Well, I've done your dirty work for you. It's time for you to get off your duffs and get the show on the road! *You* have to make whatever good is going to come of this. I gotta tell you: It was hard coming up with this idea, and it took a lot of effort to keep it under wraps until it was ripe. I'm not sure I can pull off another chance like this for you. So grab it while it's hot!"

Which brings us right back home to us and what we do with our lives.

The choice goes like this:

a) We can step out of our own personal business-as-usual so we can respond really creatively to this situation, or

b) We can wait until the situation is worse and we have less time, fewer resources, and more chaos and barely enough time and energy to keep our heads above water.

That's the carrot, and that's the stick.

My personal conclusion—just for me, mind you (you'll have to figure out what's right for you)—is that it is time to pour all the life energy I can muster into this one, starting yesterday.

I've spent my whole life trying to change the world for the better, usually with little result. And from where I sit, it seems to me that the carrots and sticks don't get much bigger than this. Massive change is on the launching pad, and the countdown has begun. I see no better investment of me, anywhere. I realize there are no guarantees, but I'm determined to do the best I can.

How about you? #

Y2K and Our Big Bet

By Larry Shook

The premise of Y2K seems almost too ridiculous to accept. A simple technical flaw with the potential to, at worst, jeopardize civilization, at best cost twice as much as the Vietnam War to fix? Please. It's like one of those adrenaline-flushed movie previews Hollywood is so fond of.

Still, skepticism is good and if, like many of us, you're still not persuaded of the need for rapid personal and community actions by the articles you've already read, there's only one more suggestion that occurs to me. Review the proceedings of a Y2K conference hosted by the Center for Strategic & International Studies on June 2, 1998 in Washington, D.C. and broadcast on C-Span. It's easy to get both a videotape and transcript of this conference, and I urge readers to do this in order to come to their own conclusions. For thirty years CSIS has been a sober voice of scholarship and reason in a puzzling and often dangerous world. It's as reputable a think tank on public affairs as you will find anywhere. The views expressed at the June 2 briefing are as sobering as anything you'll ever likely hear. For the purposes of this discussion, here's a brief summary:

- "The world is virtually doomed to have major Y2K problems."
- Fixing Y2K in time is impossible. We have to do something else.
- World leaders should plan for Y2K as though it were an approaching war.
- While impact from Y2K is inevitable, the scope is not. With immediate contingency planning, the disruption might be held to significant but manageable. Without such immediate action, Doomsday scenarios are possible.
- At risk are energy supplies, food supplies, transportation, financial systems, general government services (including defense), and general business activity.
- The U.S. probably leads the world in Y2K preparations, but

the U.S. is the most vulnerable, too.

- Our present absence of readiness is such that, "If tomorrow were 1/1/2000, our economy wouldn't grind to a halt, it would snap to a halt."
- Famine in the United States beginning in the year 2000 is possible.
- Individual survival initiatives are pointless and will make matters worse. Panic, start stocking your own pantry and arm yourself if you wish, but that will only make your own and everyone else's problems worse. This is a community challenge for which there will be community solutions or none at all. Translation: the best way to help yourself is to help your community.
- Individuals and communities should demand far better government attention to Y2K than they have so far received at the local, state and federal levels. The current lack of leadership compounds the possibility of a Titanic scenario. Citizens should contact government representatives immediately, request that Y2K contingency planning begin now, and that regular public progress reports be issued.
- While government is crafting its response, every citizen should get involved in community contingency planning immediately.
- At its heart, Y2K is not a technology problem. It's a "human factors" problem.
- "Don't panic, but don't spend too much time sleeping, either."

THIS PRESENTATION was moderated by former senior *Newsweek* editor Arnaud deBorchgrave. The keynote speaker was U.S. Sen. Robert Bennett (R-Utah), chairman of the Senate's special committee on the Y2K problem. (He's the one who cautioned against sleep.) Among the distinguished panelists were Dr. Edward Yardeni, chief economist of Deutsche Morgan Grenfell and one of the world's most respected economic authorities (Yardeni's the one who says that, without effective action, Doomsday and famine are possible), and such members of the technological priesthood as author Peter de Jager, former Royal Air Force intelligence expert Alan Simpson, Keith Rhodes of the General Accounting Office, and software expert Bruce Webster.

For your own video, call C-SPAN, 1-800-277-2698 and order tape #106506, the three-hour 6/2/98 broadcast. The tape costs $90, plus $75 for three-day shipping if you're in a hurry (normal shipping takes three weeks). You could chip in with friends to get this tape immediately, share it, discuss it, see if you can get your local public access station to air it. Anyone who watches this tape without being concerned, it seems to me, should probably just stock the cupboard with gin and get comfortable.

If you don't want to buy the tape but if you have access to the World Wide Web, go to the CSIS web page: www.csis.org/ and open up "CSIS Tackles Millennium Computer Crisis." Then go to the "June 2 Conference" and open "Conference Transcripts." You can print out everything that was said, photocopy it, share it with friends.

On the CSIS web page, I also recommend the "Y2K Crisis Links" and "Y2K Web Site." Check out "Dr. Yardeni's Economics Network." On August 19, 1998 Dr. Yardeni will host "Global Y2K Action Day, T-500 and Counting." Track the proceedings.

To understand the school of thought that Y2K can't be fixed, open "Year 2000 and Euro: IT Challenges of the Century." Then read "Routine That Became a Meltdown." It's a chilling report of a manufacturing test in Australia that suggests humanity's sudden vulnerability to this strange new bug.

Well, fine. So what's the average grudging computer user like me to do? I just can't shake the implausibility of it all, and I know from conversations with friends and family that I'm not alone.

That said, as of today I'm taking Y2K seriously. It's July 29, 1998. I hope that on July 29, 2000 I'm able to look back on this moment and feel foolish for my worry. Right now, however, the chorus of concern has simply grown too loud for me to ignore. People I have every reason to trust say that anything from the equivalent of storm surf to a tidal wave may be coming. Do I stand on the beach and wait to see if they're right?

This is the crisis of choice we all face: do we mill around in disbelief, or do we take action? And what should we do?

The second question is the most complicated, but before considering it, just ask yourself this: is it better to have an emergency plan and no emergency, or an emergency and no plan?

I find that my own instincts are not to chop wood, stockpile food and head for the hills (though I've always dreamed of a country life). My decision is to do what I'm doing at this moment: facilitate the flow of information and head for the town halls, to join with others and try to figure out what to do.

Together. *E pluribus unum.*

At this moment, my problem as an American citizen is that a credible group of leaders has gotten out ahead of the White House,

"We need to alarm the public."

—Dr. Edward Yardeni

the business community and the financial community and declared... well, a national emergency. Surely, they have not done this lightly. The Center for Strategic and International Studies went to the trouble to create a high-profile national podium for comments like these by individuals of stature:

"[If you see that you can't fix Y2K in 18 months] you can begin to spend 18 months developing contingency plans that will see to it that you at least not shut down... When people say to me, 'Is the world going to come to an end [because of Y2K],' I say I don't know. I don't know whether this will be a bump in the road—that's the most optimistic assessment of what we've got, a very serious bump in the road—or whether this will, in fact, trigger a major worldwide recession with absolutely devastating economic consequences in some parts of the world." —Senator Robert Bennett

" 'The fundamentals are fine!' is the cry from Wall Street. They are oblivious to the fact that the wheels are going to fall off the cart... We are headed for the first turn in the road in this information highway, and we forgot to put in a steering wheel... We have both the ability and the capability—we even have the resources necessary to fix this problem.... What we lack is the management will and courage to face this problem square in the eye and deal with it. And until we find that courage the people who recommend that you head for the hills may be the ones with the answer." —Peter de Jager

"I am an optimist on Y2K. I expect that we will hear good news. But I also think there will be significant vital systems that will not be operational in time, and I think these will have a domino effect on the rest of us who think that we have fixed our system, and as a result I think there will be some really significant disruptions on a global basis. So I'm an optimist but I'm also an alarmist on the Year 2000 problem... Could it be six months of major disruptions to our computer systems? Absolutely. Could it be an entire year? Absolutely... The April 27 [1998] *Fortune* magazine... quoted the chief information officer worldwide of General Motors saying there are 'catastrophic problems' in every GM plant... What's really missing here is leadership on this issue... We desperately need to have leaders tell the public what's really going on... We need to alarm the public. You're not going to panic anybody a year and a half in advance of the problem. You can alarm the public, and then the public will make sure that politicians, the business leaders do everything in their power to fix this problem. If we don't let the public in on this problem, then they will panic sometime next year... I'm not a doomsayer. I'm not talking about the end of life on planet Earth. But... if we continue to pretend there isn't a problem coming, Doomsday scenarios are conceivable... We have to tell the public, 'Some things you depend on may simply not work...' The contingency plan is to prepare people for the fact that certain products, services and information that they really need aren't going to be available. You're going to have to conduct your business, your life, without some things for a while... We have to do two things. We have to operate on two levels. One is, we have to make it *the* number one priority—stop everything else and fix the problem! And two, we have to prepare for the fact that we're not going to completely fix it. There are going to be failures. And we have to reconstruct as quickly as possible. We have to minimize the panic, because the panic will make the crisis much worse than otherwise it needs to be." —DR. EDWARD YARDENI

By the time this book went to press, the White House, industry and Wall Street were all still pretty quiet. Why?

The CSIS panelists and other close observers of Y2K (see Douglass Carmichael's piece on page 60) say this is because the politicians are waiting for November elections to pass, and industry and Wall Street are more concerned with legal liability and stock prices than the survival of the republic. (Panelist Alan Simpson declared that if the politicians stalled action on Y2K another six months, "then I've lost all hope.") In other words, Y2K could bring about an epic confrontation between America's most polar personality traits: self-interest and self-sacrifice. If this showdown materializes, and if the Y2K Cassandras are right, then either our finest or our darkest hour may be at hand. Whatever the case, the public is entitled to clear and persuasive official responses to CSIS's alarming declaration. Or should we just hope that this venerable old institution has unaccountably gone off its rocker?

It seems to me that Y2K confronts us with two basic problems. The first is purely practical: how do we keep the power on, food in the larder, water flowing from the tap, etc.? The second is a little more abstract: How do we talk to each other about this? If, in the end, Y2K really does cause widespread social disruption, my guess is it will have more to do with the second problem than the first. Just now, I have good friends who see in all this the unfolding of events transcribed by a fisherman 2000 years ago and foretold in the Book of Revelations. Others are reminded of the Hopi prophesies. Still others bring up the predictions of the old French physician and prophet Nostradamus. Some see Y2K as a cosmic joke. Some take the view it's just one more technological hurdle to clear, albeit a pretty big one.

Let's say the Millennial Bug actually has become the Millennial Bomb. What we know from the experience of war is that it's pretty hard to bomb a society out of existence. People become resilient and selfless in the face of adversity. But of all the wars in humanity's bellicose repertoire, none is deadlier than holy war, that heartless, mindless bloodbath over meaning. This is where Y2K's test, if it comes, could be most severe. We must create a compass of common values and shared hopes—and quickly—if we are to find our way in what could be an altered social and economic landscape. How do we go about that?

Senator Bennett has set seven priorities for preventing Y2K from unraveling society. They involve preserving the utilities, safeguarding telecommunications, keeping transportation running, holding the financial system together, maintaining general government services (defense included), sustaining general business activity, averting an orgy of self-defeating litigation.

Look at it this way. Assume Y2K really can knock out the power grid. If the power goes, we get cold, we lose water (it's pumped and filtered with electricity), we get sick, we quickly overload health care. But between now and 2000, is it possible to accelerate new power sources that deregulation of the electric utility industry has launched already? The answer depends on who you ask.

This has to do with the creation of decentralized, micro-grid sources of energy. I asked Amory Lovins, one of the world's foremost authorities on this subject, if he thought it could be done. If anyone's hunch on this seemed worth betting on it's Lovins'.

"Yes," he said. "It wouldn't be a trivial undertaking, but it could be done."

I took that as good news. Gearing up the industrial might that won World War II wasn't trivial either, but it was done.

Twenty-two years ago, in his influential treatise on "soft energy" in one of the world's most prestigious journals, *Foreign Af-*

fairs, Lovins argued that the global petroleum-based energy system would inevitably change as oil supplies dwindle. He advocated turning to the abundant supplies of much cleaner natural gas as a transitional fuel while sustainable technologies—photovoltaics in conjunction with less wasteful energy practices, etc.—were put in place.

Today, the electric utility industry is following Lovins' advice by turning to small, scattered natural gas turbine generators as a far more economical and reliable source of power than the old, hideously expensive coal, nuclear and hydro plants. Y2K or no, these power sources are already revolutionizing America's energy system. As this book goes to press, Lovins reports, such companies as Capstone and Allied Signal are shipping the new generation of micro-turbines. Can this process be expedited, coupled to Y2K-resistant sources of natural gas, as part of a rational contingency plan? Again, Lovins thinks it's possible. I asked if his Rocky Mountain Institute, one of the nation's top independent energy consulting organizations, could help organize such a conversion.

"We could help," he said, "but the American Public Power Association is in a far better position to do that."

But Mike Hyland, director of engineering for the American Public Power Association in Washington, D.C., the national trade representative of more than 2,000 state and local government-owned electric utilities, disagreed with Lovins.

"It took a hundred years to build the grid," he said. "You're not going to replace it between now and 2000. Besides, this isn't a fuel source problem. It's an embedded problem."

Beyond that, however, Hyland said he doesn't think widespread Y2K disruption of America's electricity is likely. Reason: while Y2K is a new specific problem, it's only a modern variation on the electric industry's oldest nemesis. It fits in the category of "things that can disrupt the flow of juice." Hyland says the industry owes its second-by-second existence to its ability to respond to such events, and he's confident, based on polling his members, that the industry's history, coupled with its intensive Y2K efforts, make widespread outages unlikely.

"If you're asking if your TV could go black on New Year's eve 2000 while you're watching the ball in Times Square go down, yes. A drunk on his way home from a party could hit a utility pole, a squirrel could get fried in the lines, the wind could blow, a blizzard could take out your power. Or a Y2K glitch somewhere near you could interrupt your service. But I don't think it will stay out for long. If you're asking me if I'll be on an airplane or a train, or in an elevator in January 2000, no way."

How to reconcile Hyland's optimism with references #16 and #17 in Dacia Reid's piece on page 84, I leave to you.

After loss of power, of course, loss of food supply would also cause an instant emergency. When Dr. Yardeni warns of the possibility of famine, it's because the ability to pump and distribute fuel is also vulnerable to the defective microchips in the nation's computer systems. If you lose transportation you quickly lose groceries (see "A Big Grocer's Y2K Nightmare," page 78). So what about food production?

Many agricultural experts have warned for years that despite the impressive technological achievements of modern society, never in history has the average human been so vulnerable to starvation. There are several reasons for this. One is the staggeringly destructive impact of modern agriculture. According to some experts, chemical and mechanized cultivation wastes so much soil that by 2025 the earth will no longer have enough of the precious commodity to support its human population. Other forecasts allow as much as a century of remaining soil, but the result's the same. This has nothing to do with Y2K.

Another reason for humanity's present food danger is the high-tech nature of modern farming. Old-fashioned open-pollinated plants have been replaced by hybrids. The old plants are lusty rascals, yielding a comically extravagant surplus of seeds, constantly renewing their own source. The new ones are sterile and reproduce by fragile industrial processes only. Moreover, modern agriculture is dependent on oil and the microchip. Oil makes the pesticides and herbicides that kill the bugs and weeds lured by monoculture. The chemical fertilizers on which the artificial plants depend are made from oil. It fuels the trains and trucks that keep the cities stocked with their three-days' supply of food. And of course, microchips control the rails by which much of the food comes to town.

Because of this untenable state of affairs, since the 1970s a global movement for sustainable and urban agriculture has steadily gathered momentum. If you can use the World Wide Web, type in "sustainable agriculture" and see what comes up. You will see the unmistakable outlines of a life-saving revolution waiting, vibrating, to happen. You will see, for instance that Canada has an "Office of Urban Agriculture," (www.cityfarmer.org/urbagnotes1.html), devoted to teaching society to produce food outside its door instead of three thousand miles away. You will see the National Agricultural Library maintains an Alternative Farming Systems Information Center (www.nal.usda.gov/afic), and that the U.S. Dept. of Agriculture mounts a Sustainable Agriculture Network. Similarly, the Agricultural Cooperative Extension Service in every community (www.e-answers.org) represents a local food-growing brain trust waiting to be tapped. You will see that there is an American Community Gardening Association (http://communitygarden.org/acga.htm) that identifies an army of expert food growers—and food-growing advisors—in every city. You will learn that Ecology Action's classic treatise on calorie production, *How to Grow More Vegetables Than You Ever Thought Possible on Less Land Than You Can Imagine,* is now in its fifth edition, published in eight languages, over 350,000 copies in print. (The book's *real* title, author John Jeavons wanted me to note, is found on the inside cover: *How to Grow More Vegetables* Fruits, Nuts, Berries, Grains and Other Crops...* because that's what it's really about.)

The news from alternative agriculture is that nothing on earth is more needless than famine. A world is possible that is a far more abundant than the one we know.

But can we accelerate alternative agriculture in time to make a difference for Y2K?

Canada's City Farmer is the world center for urban agriculture information. If people in the cities began working together immediately, I asked Mike Levenston, its executive director, could an alternative food supply be in place by 2000?

It's a bad news/good news situation, he answered. Or maybe the other way around, depending on how you see things.

"The bad news," said Levenston, "is that it takes time to grow food. You can't just turn it on. You can't grow food in a panic. It takes planning. If people don't really believe that Y2K can disrupt food supplies, if they wait until January 2000 to see what happens, it will be too late."

Human nature makes him skeptical that people will act in time.

I understood, but that wasn't quite my question. What I wanted to know was, based on his expertise, if people believed it *was* necessary, if they took action *now*, could an adequate alternative food system be in place by 2000?

As casually as if I asked him if the sun would rise in the morning, he answered, "No problem."

The reason for his confidence? Levenston pointed out that experience from two world wars showed that massive community gardening—"garden warriors," WW II's Victory Gardeners were called—is infinitely possible. He said that urban food production long

Conventional agriculture loses six pounds of soil for every pound of food produced.

ago proved its potential, it's just been awaiting its day in the sun. "Thousands of food growing experts can be found in every city" to show the way. "The costs are negligible. A few seeds, a few simple tools. Yes, it could be done."

I asked John Jeavons the same question and he underscored Levenston's reply. Jeavons, a Yale political science graduate, executive director of California-based Ecology Action, has devoted nearly thirty years to refining his Biointensive mini-farming methods. He has been widely commended in the national media (his book, wrote *The New York Times,* is "possibly the most detailed explanation of the Intensive gardening method available.") In more than 100 countries Jeavons' methods have proven that an entire year's worth of food can be grown for one person on about 4,000 square feet. By contrast, commercial agriculture needs 22,000 to 42,000 square feet per year per person (85,000 square feet if you eat a lot of meat). Industrial farming uses 100 percent more energy than Biointensive mini-farming, 50 percent to 100 percent more purchased fertilizer and 33 percent to 88 percent more water per pound of food eaten compared with Biointensive food-raising. In the U.S., conventional agriculture loses to wind and water erosion six pounds of soil for every pound of food produced, the ultimate deficit spending. China loses 18 pounds of soil per pound of food eaten. In contrast, proper Biointensive agriculture can actually *build* the soil—up to 60 times faster than nature.

Jeavons likes to quote Will Rogers: "They're making more people every day, but they ain't makin' any more dirt." Then he notes: Biointensive practices can *build* up to 20 pounds of soil for every pound of food eaten.

Writes Jeavons: "American farmers are 'feeding the world,' but mini-farming can give people the knowledge to feed themselves."

Such knowledge was once held to be essential, and should some of the worst Y2K nightmares come to pass, that could turn out to be the case again. But whatever food crisis Y2K produces, Jeavons sees it as a variation on our present agricultural system's slow suicide.

Jeavons' methods have "done more to solve poverty and misery than anything else we've done," former U.S. Sec. of Agriculture

Robert Bergland once said.

Of course energy and food disruption are just two of the areas threatened by Y2K. There's plenty else that could go wrong, plenty that may well be responsive to prayer alone. Meanwhile, the homely chore of growing food together—civilization's very first act of community building—could prove to be a tangible form of interfaith common prayer.

In all of this, I must confess a certain bias. More reliable, more environmentally responsible sources of energy and food don't seem to me like such inconvenient things to work for. Quickly building community doesn't seem like such a bitter pill, either.

I would much rather there was no such thing as Y2K, but the truth is, at this moment I feel a little like Brer Rabbit. ("Don't throw me in that briar patch!") It's because of the way I was raised. I can't prove it to you, but I happen to *know* we can handle Y2K. I don't know that we *will*. But I know that we *can*.

I was born in 1946 and grew up in the explosive development of post-World War II San Diego. As a boy I experienced the wonder of having great golden canyons to play in. And then I knew the grief of watching them get swallowed up, one after another, by housing and shopping centers. Deep in my soul it never made sense to me.

Fortunately, my grandparents were gardeners, organic gardeners at that. While one world constantly vanished around me, another perpetually flourished. For Granddad this was a strange passion, because he had spent most of his life as a roughneck in the Texas oil fields. Dad was a Marine during World War II, and after the war he stayed in San Diego. Grandmother and Granddad moved to be near him.

Granddad took a job as a steamfitter, performing one of the most industrial of jobs by day, dropping to his knees in the dirt after work and on the weekends, making the earth bear fruit. He became an importer of ladybugs, the old oil driller. When Granddad retired he worked harder in his garden than he ever did for a paycheck. Grandmother always wore an apron and canned constantly. They were portly and looked to have been born in Beatrix Potter's imagination. Throughout my childhood I got to experience the Garden of Eden they made together. It was the most beautiful place—green avenues of avocado trees, caverns of grapes, fruit, vegetables, sweet corn, horned toads everywhere—the most delicious food, the most fragrant world, the loveliest way of life I have ever known or heard of.

Should Y2K spawn an American landscape like my grandparents', it would feel like coming home.

There's something else. Once upon a time, I experienced the edge of the end of the world. I looked over the edge.

It was the Tet Offensive in Vietnam. I was a doorgunner on a helicopter gunship. For 48 hours I didn't sleep. We took off, pointed our guns at the ground, emptied them. We had to turn off our radios, because all of Three Corps was one big tactical emergency. Guys below would scream at us to come help them, but we had to go where we were told. When we landed we could only hope that there would be more ammunition to load, more fuel to take on. All life's normal reference points were gone, only a thin line to follow. Follow the line. Keep moving, do your job, hope others do theirs, keep hoping. I saw what can be done in such a world. It's a thing of terrible beauty.

I know we can handle Y2K, no matter what. Here's how. Right now ask yourself who you really are. What really matters to you? Who do you love, and what kind of world do you want for them? Roll up your sleeves. Move your feet. Share your gifts—*your* gifts—because we all need them.

We're all of us sentenced to history and can't avoid the events that led us to where we are. But we're also held in the vise of the present, and of this we must break free. Technology expert Alan Simpson, the RAF intelligence veteran, says one reason Y2K has become the mess it has is because no one is telling the whole truth about it. The market can be a wonderful thing, but it can also represent a deadly vortex of self-interest. We must tap its energy but avoid its killing greed.

Now is the time for all good people to come to the aid of their world. What's in our hearts is about to be writ large on the page of events around us. Stand by for a spectacular movie in living color and thrilling Dolby sound.

I can think of at least three reasons to launch aggressive, compassionate, all-together-now contingency planning, and none are because of what Y2K *will* do. We don't know what Y2K will do. The experts say Y2K's impact is unknowable.

1. Y2K *might* break the systems on which life now depends. This could—let's not mince words—destroy civilization. That's what authorities like Dr. Yardeni mean when they refer to Doomsday scenarios. It's why authorities like Senator Bennett say, "Don't panic, but don't spend too much time sleeping, either."

2. The way we're living right now is deadly. It violates our principles. We don't mean to, God knows, but we're all committing "inter-generation remote tyranny." (See William McDonough's piece

on page 132.) Short-term emergency solutions of decentralized power pegged to sustainable power later, and sustainable agriculture, and local currency and vigorous community barn-building of all sorts (see Paul Glover's "Protecting Our Community from Year 2000 Computer Chaos" on page 112) not only might save our bacon, they may represent better long-term practices anyway. McDonough, I think, is right: these are the things we should be doing anyway, even if the Y2K bogeyman were nowhere around.

3. The danger of planning for an emergency that doesn't happen is nothing compared to facing a real emergency without a plan.

But the truth is, I can also think of at least two reasons not to do anything.

1. In all likelihood, emergency measures capable of saving us will forever change the way we live. If we let these big cats of change out of the bag, we may never return to the old habits that were so hard on the earth, families, children, etc. That may seem like bad news for economic interests that benefit disproportionately from those practices.

2. Y2K may fizzle. In that case we will have gone to a lot of trouble for nothing.

We can't avoid gambling. The question is, where do we want to place our bets?

Watch The Center for Strategic and International Studies tape, or read the transcript, and note how many of these sober, conservative men mention the Titanic. "This is Titanic America," declared Deutsche Morgan Grenfell's Yardeni.

The Unitarian minister from Brockton, Mass., Dacia Reid, in her piece on page 84, writes of the Titanic metaphor: "...the disaster was not that the Titanic sank. The disaster was that so many people died because of too few lifeboats, inappropriate use of what lifeboats there were, denial, inaction, and disbelief. I have a carpenter friend who says that he just can't believe that with all the materials on that ship and all the people on board that they couldn't have devised floatation platforms for virtually everyone in the two-plus hours it took that ship to sink. It would have been a lot better than having the band play on."

Wouldn't it be ironic if the tragedy of the Titanic at the beginning of this century—our ultimate metaphor for technological arrogance and vulnerability—helped civilization itself avoid the same fate at the beginning of the next century?

As I watched the CSIS Y2K conference tape, my mind leaped

back to the eruption of Mount St. Helens in southwestern Washington. I remembered a young geologist who died. He was camped across from the volcano with the best view, and on that May morning in 1980 when the mountain blew, he had time for one brief radio transmission.

"Vancouver, Vancouver! This is it!" he cried.

And then his voice was gone as half a mountain filled the sky. #

Larry Shook has been a journalist for twenty-five years. He's written for and been an editor of *San Diego Magazine* and *Seattle Weekly*. With his wife, Judy Laddon, he published *Spokane Magazine.* He was editor-in-chief of *Washington Magazine*, and has been a stringer for *The New York Times, The Washington Post, Newsweek.* His freelance magazine articles have appeared in publications as divergent as *WorldView* and *People.* Newspaper features of his have been syndicated by Pacific News Service.

Who will do what and when will they do it?

By Douglass Carmichael

The curve of intense conversations about the computational failures for 2000 is rising rapidly. As implications are becoming vivid, some people are starting—slowly at first, so as not to appear foolish or alarming, to take actions—some organizational, and some personal. It's amazing how many people respond that they will go to work on January 1st and fix the problem, imagining that the building is open, that the power works, that offices are warm, and Starbucks is still selling coffee, and they will settle down to fixing the problems that emerged over Friday night/Saturday morning. If they get pushed to think it could be worse, people imagine that they will just stay home for a few weeks, watch television, talk on the phone, play on the Internet, while the systems folks get it all back together in the depth of the winter of 2000. Or they imagine driving out to their friends' farm to avoid the mess, without realizing they will have to get past all the other cars that clog the roads and have been abandoned for lack of fuel, and whose owners wait in the road for the next hapless innocent.

Further, people imagine that the world will return to the way it was, like the great Northeast power outage of a decade or so ago. The French writer, Camus, said in the mid '40s, "It is unbearable to imagine what we will go through."

The problem is not simple. Since at least the early 1800s the culture has standardized on the two digit year.

'Twas the eighteenth of April in '75
Hardly a man is now alive
Who remembers that famous day and year...

Longfellow. Or we have examples like the Gold Rush of '49. Programmers merely continued this practice under conditions of business created by their employers, assuming that for the time being 66,

67, 68, was a sequence easy for computational devices to handle. Turns out that when that sequence goes 99, 00, weird things will, in many cases, happen. Mixing the abstraction of numbers in a piece of computer program with real time turns out to be messy at the places where the symbols are not precise or complete. Calling it a "bug" hides the full range of social responsibility for mishandling core technologies. As intellectual capital, we failed to comprehend. Most people hope to get back to "zero", making Y2K a non-event. But since that is impossible, a deeper look at causes and reactions is essential if we are to get the leverage to create a better outcome.

And we seem mostly oblivious that this is the post-Einstein, Picasso, Marx, Freud, Stravinsky, Eliot, Yeats world. To say nothing of Blake, Beethoven, Goya, or the surrealists, already a century old. We have not assimilated our art to help us understand the awkwardness of blending technology and human desires, so necessary for understanding the meaning of Y2K.

We are entering into the next major phase, after denial, of the buildup, where cross currents of proposed solutions and blame knock against each other like the waves stirred up by throwing a handful of pebbles into the same quiet pond. We will probably be entering what could be called "the time of confusion." And exhaustion. Some see in the emerging chaos the potential beauty of self-organizing systems. But this fails to assess either the huge number of failures in the implied blind evolution (cancer and health are both self-organizing), nor that the hierarchical organizations they disdain are also self organizing systems.

I personally became involved with the year 2000 issues in May 1997. I met with the CIO of one of the Northeastern states on another project. He told a few of us at drinks before a dinner that the Y2K effort would take six years of the state's IT [information technology] budget, and would still not solve the problem in time. I didn't know what that could mean and had him explain it to me. I could feel the depth of his anxiety. In the next few months I met with several clients (Fortune 100s) at a level where I could get meaningful analyses of their Y2K approaches and potential for success.

The facts were not pretty. Recent attempts to solve the Y2K problem had been failing. One of these was the use of a software package to handle all the issues. In several major cases, that software was being rejected by divisions within some major companies, because it required centralization and integration. Another was a decision to move from mainframes to LAN-based [Local Area Network computer] workstations, and then the realization it would take too much time and training to convert and still maintain operational continuity.

During this time, I was part of conversations in a futurist-oriented consulting company's Internet conversation space. There was a noticeable lack of response to what looked like an issue many of the participants would be expected to have intimate opinions about. That redoubled my need to find out what was in fact happening. I woke up early one morning in early November 1997, angry at the emerging picture, and, to clarify my own thinking, wrote the first version of this chapter and put it on my website.

I was more struck by the psychology of the various reactions to Y2K talk than by the technology failures. As you will recall, in the early days of awareness people in business, government and the press were mostly saying, "It's just hype by the consultants," followed by, "If it is a problem, with the amount of money to be made, they will fix it." The extreme conventionality of those opinions was enough to convince me there was a very powerful undercurrent of socialization going on, probably fueled by anxiety.

A small group of us gathered Dec. 31st through Jan. 1st to look at a set of scenarios a friend, David Isenberg, had put together earlier in the year based on our online discussion. That meeting only deepened the sense I had that we were dealing with a major technical problem and a major psychological experiment in social consciousness. One political person present, face red with rage, said, "If this becomes a big problem, it is all the fault of the press. Its just a question of perceptions, of perceptions!"

I was living life in parallel parts. One was my normal activities, lived in a time frame of assumed continuities, the second was in my explorations about what was really going to happen. I certainly could not integrate the two into a pragmatic series of life decisions.

Through discussions with Stuart Umpleby and the Institute for Social and Organizational Learning at George Washington University, I got invited to give a talk at Fannie Mae to the Washington Y2K community. I knew that, while my understanding was piecemeal and intellectual, this group of about 200 would give me a sense of their assessment of the problem, and this would be news to me, whatever it would be. What I felt from this group—there was an hour-long reception before the talks, which is a brilliant way to get people talking—was resignation and fear in individual conversations, which were amazingly candid, and paralysis in the larger group. I came away no longer living life on two parallel tracks, but convinced that the problem was real, and that even solving it would alter the nature of society, to say nothing of what would happen if we didn't solve it. I also was highly aware that we did not possess good facts, and that those who knew about the problems lived in a different world from those who did not.

I'd say the most common view encountered that evening was that they, as individual organizations, were in great difficulty, were not going to get the problems fixed, and in some cases had abandoned the effort. Because of issues like the "dirty" code (based on years of rewrites and patches), and buildings run by chip "enhanced" equipment from vendors that were out of business, the length of the testing periods, the cost, the need for man-years of time, while people are leaving the organizations (programmers are following markets), it looked like there was no way out.

It was also striking that while people saw the damage and inability to function in their own organizations, they had a hard time gathering what they knew into any image of what happens at the personal, societal or community level. The money motive is not sufficient to get smart about Y2K. If it were their lives, they'd be smarter about it.

The serious purpose of the evening, to think about contingency plans, showed that what organizations have meant by "contingency" (like having backups) is totally inadequate to Y2K. Here was a group that knew that their office buildings, for example, were unexamined and vulnerable, but did not take the leap to "contingency plans" involving potential failures in the surrounding institutions and communities.

There were enough horror stories to shake me up. All added to the general view that the fear down in the trenches was worse than that felt by the managers at the top, although the number of organizations whose top leadership was involved was certainly increasing. Though recognized as important, handling the social and psychological side of all this—even just having honest internal discussions—was beyond their felt sphere of competency for most.

We didn't see what would later emerge as a problem with CEOs saying to their IT director, "Tom, you're going to fix this thing, Right?!" That just leaves people more scared and confused, and less willing to talk, and the quality of internal conversation goes down, not up.

Another problem is the culture of contempt towards workers, and with them, technologists and programmers. "Our people are working on it" is not said with affection. Programmers are very distrustful of management; managers know they are disliked but haven't cared. Manufacturing environments are often hostile, and the resulting implications for Y2K compliance are not good. But to discuss these issues is to open a can of worms.

I then went to London for a week to poke around organizations there and attended a two-day workshop sponsored by GBN London. I happened to be at a large meeting of one of England's premier technology integration companies, and that night in the hotel I stepped to the crowded bar to order a malt. I was standing next to some of the top managers as they were winding down from their day, discussing Y2K. As I waited for my drink, one of them said, "Thank god we'll be retired and off playing golf by then!"

In the year that has passed since that time, the mix of opinions has changed very little. Hard facts are difficult to come by, and each day is more of the same, only more so. Our way of understanding what will happen turns out to be like reading mystery stories; you only get one piece at a time.

The simplest explanation about the inadequacy of understanding is that Y2K touches people where they have pre-formed, firm opinions. Some people's stories are about the marvels of free market and technical progress; others are about community, national and personal disappointments regarding the current status quo. Y2K ratifies existing thinking or suspicions. People are drawn to those with similar stories to tell. At the same time, facts turn out to be scarce, because, despite that we are talking about technology, the facts are much messier than anticipated by most of us. We are not taught comparative history nor systems theory, and sociological and anthropological theory are for the most part weak or unknown to the normal news-savvy public.

Through giving many seminars and workshops, I've discovered that taking a look at the buildup from now to 2000, and focusing on post-Y2K scenarios, helps people get grounded and see continuity through 2000, rather than seeing it as hitting a wall or leaping off a cliff. It helps them see why what they do now can make a difference for what kind of situation we can help create—or avoid—after 2000. Whatever the actual path Y2K takes, everyone and all organizations will be very active trying to make the best of a messy situation. Some will be self-serving, some will be socially constructive. Little actions now can have a big impact later. Stressing continuity rather than a single spike event helps people imagine a personal, institutional and social path through the events crowded around the start of 2000.

The official view of Y2K is that nothing happens till midnight

Those in the best positions to know, mostly in the core of powerful organizations, are highly motivated to keep quiet.

December 31st 1999, and then, when the phone is dead, or the traffic lights aren't working, all hell breaks loose for 48 hours. This expectation isn't realistic. At the simplest, midnight happens in other places first, and we might have news reports by mid-morning on the 31st.

But of course the problem is not just what will happen on January 1, 2000. The question is, "What will people do in anticipation, as their understanding increases?" And "When will they start doing it? "There are signs people are already on the move. North or south, buying stand-alone electric generators, holding gold or cash, thinking about food, water, health, guns. Will we get inflation or deflation? How scary, how long will it last? But above all, when will the reaction begin in perceptible doses, and how will the press react? Will they blame and amplify tensions or help the conversation and learning? These questions are increasingly on the minds of many people.

One interesting perspective is to think of the number of people who should have been involved to get Y2K basically fixed, and those who actually have been and will be.

Unlike most social movements, in this case nearly everyone will be in the conversation. We mostly need to think about how to help the conversation, not create it.

It's important to see that there is a buildup towards 2000, and lots of continuous activity afterwards. A problem that did not get fixed in the previous two years will not be fixed in a week afterwards.

Those in the best position to know, mostly in the core of powerful organizations, are highly motivated to keep quiet. First, to avoid being an internal scapegoat, and second, to avoid flagging to the outside world that their organization is one of those in trouble. The result is, we are not getting the feedback we need. Organization lawyers are now actively recommending this path to their clients, or even ordering it. A recent New York meeting of Y2K lawyers stressed protecting the client. No one raised the issue that, with organizations taking this route, society does not get the information to make decisions. A major newspaper cannot get its local electric company to tell them frankly what is likely.

I have been in meetings where the challenge goes out—"Who is compliant with robustness for 2000?"—and no one responds. The lawyers have said, make no claims, give no details; certainly you break contracts if you say you can't make it. Technical people are being told by the boss, "Do what is necessary to fix it; I am committed." But that's hard on employees who are convinced it can't be fixed, and they have no one to talk to. The "smart" ones are going to move quietly, to protect their personal and organizational strategies, and the public won't get meaningful feedback.

Those who want to hush the problem ("Don't talk about it, people will panic," and "We don't know for sure,") are having three effects. First, they are preventing a more rigorous investigation of the extent of the problem. Second, they are slowing down the awareness of the intensity of the problem as currently understood and the urgency of the need for solutions, given our current assessment of the risks. Third, they are making almost certain a higher degree of ultimate panic.

It's my judgement that the earlier we flesh out the possibilities, the quicker we mobilize efforts to solve the problem. We need to design contingency plans and alternative solutions. Finding ways to help people into the conversation is important. For those who are sure we have a problem, a word of caution: stick with the fact that we do not know, that there will be surprises, that human initiatives can have amazing effects—good and bad. In our not-knowing for sure, we can still lay out a complex vision of the range of possibilities consistent with our facts and suppositions. If we do this, people will listen. If we take a stand ahead of the facts, we stir resistance. John Koskinen, Clinton's able Y2K federal coordinator, has been quoted as saying, "We need to find the fine line between informing and panic."

The buildup towards 2000 is influenced by our guesses about what will happen. It's interesting to see how people seem to know, like a hunch at a horse race, which way it will go. The most salient fact is, we do not know and all that we do think we know could be washed out by other aspects of the problem, aspects we have not paid any attention to. For example, will the U.S. stock market go up, or down? Business failures and bank closings, electrical utilities not working, suggest down, but to the extent that the U.S. banks are seen as more compliant than European ones, cash will flow into U.S. banks and the stock market, as placeholders for wealth. The market could go to 20,000. Not only that but the market could come way down, not by lowering its dollar value but through very rapid inflation, so that the Dow remains at 10,000 while the rest of the world goes up.

You've still got your dollar value, but the value is much less. Surprises. And don't beat yourself up for not getting it right. Its too nonlinear. The secondary effects will be larger than the primary.

The main thrust of this article is to convince you that the financial game is not the only game in town, that community and society are also at risk, and the opportunities are not just business opportunities, but societal. The normal consciousness of today is indeed almost exclusively finance and business, and to the extent these arenas break down, it will shift to personal and familial survival. It's considered wisdom to say, "Y2K is not a technical problem, it's a business survival issue." (The conventionality of this language, so frequently heard, is a symptom of a complex social process.) Actually it is a technical issue, it is a business survival issue, and it is a community survival issue. Politics is asleep, and communities have disappeared, replaced by cable TV, work stress, Internet nightly vacations, and safe sex that does not require actually looking for a relationship.

Let's look at the buildup toward 2000.

Political. Clinton gives the State of the Union addresses in January 1999 and January 2000. But there are Congressional elections (and many state and local) in November 1998. Forbes is already running on a Y2K agenda, and Gingrich has made strong statements. Gore's fate might hang on how he handles Y2K. The first primary is in January of 2000.

I believe that sometime probably late in 1998 there will be a move by the G8 and a number of multinational corporations to try to "manage" the Y2K response. So far so good, but when it gets tied to emergency measures and threatens non-included corporations, it could turn into a giant gridlock. This in turn would stir more political activity. We have just seen a number of state legislatures already vote to protect themselves, while in California a bill failed that would have protected corporations. There will be further "amnesty" legislation around legal damages, but they will raise such deep constitutional issues that we can expect no action. It's possible that people and businesses will push for nationalizing the electrical utilities, because that may be the only way to get accurate information on progress towards compliance. The range is great, and we can expect surprises.

Economic. Movement of the stock market. Most people expect a break downwards. The economy is not in such good shape anyway, independent of Y2K. There are areas of worldwide over-production, cars being one, and we still have a way to go before we can assess the effects of the Asian crisis. But the market might stay up, either because of Asian and European money entering, or because of rapid inflation where a steady market means an actual decline in real value. We might also see increased market turbulence with no emerging trend. There is likely to be a feeding frenzy around assets of failing or perceived-to-be failing companies. Some will actually announce that they have not and will not make the investment. The values of perceived-to-be-compliant companies, aided by nearly mythic statements like, "The big companies are way ahead" (implying that all little or mid-sized ones are not), will affect share prices unfairly.

Will business itself decline? Not completely, for sure. Some business will do very well till 2000. One prediction is that we can, independent of specific Y2K effects, expect an increase in market because of hoarding and replacement, of about 2%, with a corresponding post-Y2K time-limited crash of perhaps 5% based on inventory reduction. The interesting part is what happens post-Y2K.

Media: A rapid rising curve of media attention will keep rising, though it may peak in about early 1999. While it rises, scapegoats will be necessary to keep the focus off markets and managerial decisions. But the press will need to deal with the question, how did we get into this mess? Blaming programmers and IT managers is likely to be one major route. Worldwide criticism of the U.S. may grow intense. What will be the counter reaction? We will watch the sequence of cover stories. There will be a major movie release in fall of 1998; programs like Meet the Press and Sixty Minutes will explore the issues confrontationally.

Societal: Churches, universities, non-profits, National League of Cities, trade associations, each can be expected to come into the conversation vigorously. We are beginning to see special panels and presentations at already scheduled national meetings. This will increase the demands to "do something." What we will notice is that there will be many voices, but very few that even attempt to speak for society as a whole (or even community in the holistic sense). We have lost much of our social capital around these concepts.

Security: Security efforts will tend to highlight the degree to which we are a stratified society. Threat to property will get confused with shifting values because of market reevaluations. But as the situation begins to look worse, the debate around the deployment of the National Guard, Reserves and regular military will get intense. The wild card is, many of those people may have other things to do and not show up, and the communications infrastructure of those groups is threatened. But it will be hard for units to focus against those they identify with. We can expect an effort to mobilize to guard major corporate and governmental assets, and middle-class communities. We can also expect geographically coherent communities, mostly towns, to mobilize local walkie-talkie based security in the event of difficulties from outside.

Community. We can expect intense analysis of town/city vulnerability to outages or shortfalls of power, water, heat, food, health and transportation. This could lead to rethinking local dependence and a rethinking of how communities might be somewhat more self-reliant, with local production. During the pre-Year 2000 period we can expect many community meetings, sorting out power and politics, finance and people. This will absorb a tremendous amount of time and effort, and could possibly be deeply fruitful for rediscovering community.

Personal. Once most of us get past the, "I'll go south" (or the family will) by realizing that everyone else will have the same thought, we can start turning to others for advice and solutions. Jefferson's *Pursuit of Happiness* referred to "happenings," and the range of roles an adult plays in society. The more roles the "happier." In recent years roles have collapsed into work and family. The individual impoverishment for most of us has been noticeable, regretted, and paralyzing. New levels of community activity will lead to individuals doing their personal thinking and looking for ways to participate. The implications are profound, and are already to be seen.

It's clear that all these buildups towards 2000 are influenced by imagined outcomes at 2000.

There seem to be two main directions for the path through 2000. That we spend the money and get it fixed, or that we spend the money and don't. In both cases our investment strategy should have the same underlying structure, just more intense as we see that we may get major systems failures.

First is the Long Boom direction, stated boldly by Peter Schwartz in *Wired* magazine. The basic idea: this free market economy can grow at 6% for 25 years. While the Asian crisis came only a few weeks after the scenario was published, its underlying logic, with some fixes, is still not totally implausible. Its momentum, already underway for the last ten years, implies that, for Y2K we have a large problem that is solved with lots of cash. This means worldwide maybe one trillion dollars spent between now and, say, September 1999. This alone, as we already can see, is requiring a major effort and enabling legislation. It is requiring a worldwide mobilization of people that can be likened to a community effort to pile cement bags to hold back the flood, but with the technical and managerial complexity of a dozen or more Manhattan Projects. There are emerging more and more serious, hectic, hysterical and face-saving efforts. We can expect all these to increase, with still unpredictable results, including some that work. Don't underestimate human ingenuity.

If we add the time spent in things like reading this article, conversations over lunch, anxious meetings among top managers, then the real cost of merely fixing the problems will be three times the one trillion dollars. It is taking up the social channels as well as paid work time. Think of the cost of canceling planned New Year's celebrations for 1999.

But it is not all just lost dollars: it's also stimulating a shifting economy that has value of its own. It certainly contributes to productivity and GNP, at the same time it takes money away from where it would have been spent. A true estimate requires putting the two patterns of spending into a comparative analysis.

Most importantly, Y2K may trigger rethinking in the proper use of technology for the quality of life and community, and simultaneously releasing tremendous worldwide economic activity to actually get there. What Y2K does to the original Long Boom scenario is add the community and quality of life correction that was absent in that "more for us and let them eat trickle down" approach in the exuberant "Silicon Valley for the world" model.

The second direction, if the fixing doesn't work, is a major collapse of key infrastructure: financials, telecom, transportation, utilities, food, water, health. During World War II all the major infrastructure in every European country remained intact. Even with the collapse of the Soviet Union, the major infrastructure of food, water, power, and transportation continued. We can also expect threats to cash, the paper value of wealth, and markets. The psychological and social consequences require some major acts of imagination to begin to get the picture of the consequences. (In my mind I see Goya's sketches of the civil war in Spain.)

The year 2000 problem also resonates with weak markets, overproduction, increasing disparities of have/have-nots, and the increasing dependency on technology everywhere. This has the makings of a very dangerous situation, leading to widespread chaos and anxiety. There are potentially three emerging responses from the social side. And it is the social side that shows a weakness in our social imagination. We seem to be able to talk about the threat to financial institutions and businesses, but we seem to lack a sympathetic imagination when it comes to people, communities, children, sick, poor or suburban; all threatened to the core of their being. Our over-reliance on the technology has made us blind to people.

Of the three potential directions, two are quite negative: the threat of rapid deprivation of scarce reserves, with people scared, angry, hungry and cold, could lead us either to centralized techno-fascism or local Mafia-like tough guy control.

Is normal government out of the picture? Can large government cohere? Can the multinationals organize an alternative? The answers are unclear, but they are generally part of one side of the equation. Those with power will attempt to preserve that power and let those without fail. But the basic distribution of goods—the simple things, like water, food and energy (heat and light and cars)—are likely to fall out of their control. The breakup of the Soviet Union is a good model to learn from where, with a break in the official system, the black market emerged as the new legitimate form of market and governance.

A more positive possibility is that we get a new form of governance through an improvised Internet that supports a democratic and more community-based society, making good use of distributed light technologies, such as the Internet at the core, with cellular phones, solar energy, and new forms of locally producing biotechnology for food and fuel. This will require lots of effort and clarity of purpose. A solution that helps distribute goods and maintains an ethical social platform, that is democratic and compassionate, is going to be hard to achieve.

So you can see why I think it is so important to focus on a coherent community-based response that offers something to people, not just to business systems.

One of the most helpful images and supporting analyses to help people see the context of what might happen, are the four scenarios derived from looking at the two major unknowns: 1) will failures be significantly interdependent, and 2) will society hold together?

Each of the following four scenarios can be characterized in a sentence.

The *Official Future* is what our organizations and leadership are mostly saying: a few failures, no social impact or reaction, keep to your oars.

Smoke in the Theater is the media-induced panic to a few important but not interlinked failures. The reaction causes more and more problems to emerge as people abandon their positions.

The *Millennial Collapse* is terrible, and in a just-in-time, no-storage world where half the world's population of six billion are in cities, over-crowded, dependent on transportation and communica-

We could not rule out that social collapse would turn us into a Rwanda, a Bosnia, a worldwide spasm of social reaction grasping for power and control.

tions and the goodwill of those in the supporting infrastructure—a real catastrophe is possible. Perhaps we can let ourselves be motivated by an awareness of this dark scenario. We could not rule out that social collapse would turn us into a Rwanda, a Bosnia, a worldwide spasm of social reaction grasping for power and control. In such a world, a loss of half the population is not out of the question.

It's sufficient motive to mobilize us toward the fourth scenario, *Human Spirit and the Spirit of Community.*

From a goals and values point of view, this is the most hopeful of all. So social survival is the catalyst. Now we start to get smart.

Based on current realities, I think we can exclude the isolated failures scenarios except as teaching aids to help bring people into the conversation who are new to it. Of course, if the wind shifts, we may need to bring them back, but as of now, I think we deal with the last scenario, where we accept interconnected failures as given.

Taking a broader view leads to rethinking investment. Some of what is being spent now towards fixing the problems ought to be targeted towards having in place what we will need on January 1st to be able to repair what didn't work.

In this process, some technologies will be more attractive than others. Y2K will nudge us towards lighter, swifter, more distributed technologies, such as cellular, fuel cells, and biotech for local crop production, things that are available now but need more investment and/or more market robustness. We come out of Y2K different than we go in, despite the prevailing expectation of simple "fix it" and "recovery" periods.

Our investment strategies now can greatly affect our communities.

Paul Ray argues that 45 million Americans, whom he calls the Cultural Creatives (the other two groups being the Traditionals and the Moderns), are ready for more quality of life: relationships, leisure, environment, and they would choose less work to get it if they could. These people seem ready to grasp the emerging Y2K investment strategy without needing to develop new attitudes: they are ready. They just need to see the logic.

Governance. It's fairly clear that some federal, state and local agencies and functions will be hard hit. Congress, and other legislative bodies in the states, are likely to take the opportunity, in the triage language of today, to cease to fund many of their functions. We then have the possibility of a revitalized public, accountable by geographical location, cost-effective investment, and an emerging new governance to support the Y2K environment.

These concepts would replace a bump and cash drain with a coherent strategy that links current actions through 2000 towards a future that can integrate not only technology choice, new governance, community focus and those who desire a better coherence to the human side of cultural choices, but also environmental reason, manufacturing for zero emissions, saner transportation policy for ground and air. The result would be a single, coherent, fairly loose coalition of interests, interests that are not deeply antagonistic to each other.

There will be extraordinary personal pain and fear on the part of everyone, without exception, regardless of which scenario plays out. Asset preservation will appear first, before community or personal survival is taken seriously. Hopefully we can get past that as people recognize the power of an integrated approach reaching from now towards a future that makes both technical and human sense. The coming shift of production towards local communities makes such a possibility a little more likely.

Given this picture of unfolding difficulties, what do we do? There are several reasonable courses of action. We must proceed on multiple paths simultaneously. I propose that we work in parallel along the following lines.

1) Try to fix the current systems and their interdependencies. Try to hold together and repair as much as we can. This might save 70 percent of the overall system.

2) Simultaneously build the B-system, an interconnection of systems that are guaranteed totally clean. This might include 25 percent of existing fully repaired systems, tested and interconnected by December 1999. This would give us a lower limit to failure. Harlan Smith of *Computer Professionals for Social Responsibility* calls this "austere infrastructure."

3) Develop contingency plans, including the preparation of new legislation, so there can be a debate on what would be tolerable and what would be intolerable and under what conditions. There will be waves of attempted and failed legislation, failing because it stirs too much resistance or is unconstitutional. The second and third waves of legislation will be more, not less, radical.

4) Like the air raid practices of World War II, we need to prac-

tice soon, cold turkey, for a week, one at time, without banks, electricity, water or food. The population needs to practice, to get tough.

5) Do all we can to create participatory local community response as a protection against survivalist reactions and strong-arm local control. Communities can hold open space meetings (large circle, open agenda, to create breakout groups of their choice, self selection) to create self managing, emergent structures, to meet basic needs (food, heat, water, sanitation, then health and meaningful activity). We need to make sure that we are in the self-organizing mode and do not allow "committees of concern" to become local un-elected Soviets.

6) Use the media to create images of survivalist/starvation vs. vital community cooperation to rework local production and distribution. I can image TV spots that show the situation and the response of the mean-spirited bad guys and the community-spirited good guys, with the clear implication that playing together gives a much greater sense of success than playing isolated survivalist.

7) Use advertising agencies to create interesting, even fun, informative awareness of the problem. Being creative about it will shift the perception from boring and scary, to scary and interesting.

8) Stress actions now, given probable major failures, that can help create a very attractive post-Y2K community, businesses and governance. Show people the need for cooperation instead of isolated gun and bunker solutions. Help the creation of new market mechanisms at the local level. There will be rapid innovation, some good, some monopolistic and exploitative. Recognize that, while all this is "terrible," there are also opportunities to radically rethink technology, the place of money, the opportunities for community, art, relationships. It's important to look for ways of bringing forward every positive image of a new community. We might get a more individual and community-focused future. No longer so much abstract market and consumption, but the graceful use of technology and education to meet human needs and leave people in the foreground, not marginalized as in the current technology/market/career mix.

9) Doing all we can to get people employed will be as critical as food and heat. Creating kits and printing pamphlets to encourage people to knit, peel potatoes, plant seeds, whatever, will be important and needs to be done on a massive scale. There is some hope in this, and it's fascinating to work towards. Meaningful contribution is the key, ASAP. A person who works on flood control told me that, "We arrive with cans of paint and brushes, and organize the teenag-

ers to paint the mailboxes as soon as the water recedes." The message is obvious. Hunger, plus nothing helpful to do, supports survivalist undermining of the social fabric.

10) It will be important to maintain the loop between human effort and meeting needs. We'll want local mechanisms of exchange, which might mean local printed money, the value of which is locally determined (this based on the likelihood of rapid inflation in federal dollars as federal check writing quickly outstrips revenue). [Ithaca Hours is a good example. See Paul Glover's piece on page 112. — J.L.]

11) Talk to friends and relatives, get them aware, get them talking, thinking. This in itself sets a community tone.

I AND MANY OTHERS look at Y2K as part of the flawed integration of technology with society and with the real human beings. People are dependent on technical systems that have grown like the water systems of ancient Mesopotamia, where the extended infrastructure to support agriculture used all the surplus to feed the workers maintaining the system. Eventually overwhelmed, the system collapsed. Owner greed pushed the extensions of the water systems further than made sense.

We have learned a good deal about how to make large-scale community conversations useful. Talking about scenarios is one of those ways. The serious possibility of failures impels us to discuss contingencies. But contingencies for what? We really don't yet know. We see a tendency to gridlock in our organizations as people see that budget needs may require crossing boundaries to get the needed cash. Planning stirs up issues around turf and budget. Talking about scenarios—that is, some plausible images of the future beyond what we know for sure—gets people engaged with much less anxiety. Having looked at scenarios in cross-organizational groups, we can then talk more fully about what we should do.

We need to be doing this anyway, independent of Y2K. Y2K just ups the urgency.

As the poet said, "We live in fierce times." Or as James Michener said when asked about the future, "First, I'm against it, and second, I don't want to miss it."

It may be just the challenge we need to get us thinking more about better ways to integrate technology into human life and society. #

NOTES
More at http://tmn.com/y2k or email me at doug@tmn.com.
Started and stimulated by Don Michael, whose *Planning to Learn, Learning to Plan,* is seminal on the difficulties of planning.
The scenario quadrant was first proposed by David Isenberg (Copyright 1997), www.isen.com, and amplified in a workshop Dec 31-Jan 1 1997/1998. The "Who will do what" paper was written by Carmichael in November 1997.
The Collapse of Complex Societies, Joseph Tainter, Cambridge University Press, 1988.
The Great Wave, David Hackett Fischer, Oxford University Press, 1996.

As an undergraduate at Caltech, **Douglass Carmichael** had the good fortune of meeting Maslow, Oppenhiemer and John Weir, the combination leading him to Berkeley, to psychology, philosophy and anthropology. He got his doctorate in developmental psychology and the issues of the origins of knowledge, the workings of the mind, language and culture.

He did post-doctoral work at Harvard's Center for Cognitive Studies and, having dealt with the more rational side of knowing, he then went to Mexico to study psychoanalysis with Erich Fromm and his school. From Mexico he went to Santa Cruz as a professor in History of Consciousness, and Psychology, and established a relationship with Nevitt Sanford at Berkeley and Michael Maccoby then at the Center for Advanced Studies in the Behavioral Sciences. Both of these teachers were looking at the relationship of psychology to society.

He was an associate at the Institute for Policy Studies and clinical professor of psychology in the graduate program at Catholic University in Washington D.C.

During this time he also taught at Children's Hospital, St. Elizabeth's Hospital, and continued clinical studies at the Washington School of Psychiatry, in the Advanced Psychotherapy Program, where he was later a professor for a number of years. He was a Harvard Research Fellow at the Harvard Program on Technology and Society and worked with Michael Maccoby on the development of Fromm's theory of social character.

He participated in the Volvo experiments in Europe, and worked with Einar Thorsrud and the Norwegian Work Research Institute. He was fortunate to meet Erich Trist, who visited his project on participatory work at the World Bank.

For extended periods of time Carmichael visited Russia, India, Japan and North Africa, and later, Java and Bali. He was the founding president of the Washington Conservatory of Music and on the boards of the Forum for Humanities and Psychiatry, and the British Institute in America.

With children grown, his consulting increased and he joined the School for Management and Strategic Studies in La Jolla, Calif., and got involved in early efforts using computers online for collegial work environments with a group of sixty executives and thinkers looking at world strategic issues. He consulted at Bell Labs where he used a new dialup asynchronous conferencing capacity to support a major change effort at administration services. Fascinated with the technology and its ability so enhance learning environments and change efforts, he became president of Metasystems Design Group, which he left in 1998 to start a new company, Shakespeare and Tao Consulting (http://tmn.com/shakespeareandtao).

A Big Grocer's Y2K Nightmare

Anonymous

I'm the manager of a grocery and drug combination store which is part of one of the top five grocery chains in the country. The store is on track to do about $40 million this year, well above the industry average and close to the top of my division. We employ over 200 people, most of them full-time. Each week we strive to satisfy over 50,000 customers. I hope this establishes my credentials. For perhaps obvious reasons, I'd rather not say where or with whom I work.

The closing months of 1999 should be interesting. I expect to see a great deal of panic buying, particularly in the last few weeks of December.

That's not difficult to foresee. How well our supply network, both company warehouses and local vendors, can keep pace with the increased demand remains to be seen.

In any typical week, we're out of stock on somewhere around 2% of the SKUs. Some grocery stores are higher, few are lower. By 12/1/99, I would expect that figure to rise to 40%. By the end of the month, I would not be surprised to see out-of-stocks at 75%, and whatever remains will be the slower-moving items. Keep in mind, too, that that could mean three to four times my typical sales for that week, which is already the best or second best of the year. That means extremely crowded aisles and extremely long lines.

Beware.

On 01/01/2000, we will be at the mercy of our electricity and telecommunications providers. Should the electricity fail, our backup generators should last us around six hours. During that time, power is routed to only the registers (minus the POS [Point of Sale] scanning system), the pharmacy computer system, and a few lights scattered around the store. Freezers are down, HVAC is down, all other electrical systems are down.

After six hours we are completely in the dark. The next time you are at your local grocery store, take note of the lighting. Most stores, mine included, have a lot of glass at the front end of the store and nowhere else. If the store were to go black, the back half of the store

Without power, we would become something like a really big, really empty, really dark, and possibly really cold indoor farmers' market.

as well as the side perimeters are virtually unnegotiable without a flashlight.

The registers would be completely useless. Imagine how long the lines would be if we had to run around getting price checks on every single item, hand-write receipts, manually calculate sales tax and total, etc. Some problems could be alleviated somewhat: hand-ticket the merchandise (extremely time-consuming and virtually impossible given our present payroll constraints), ignore the sales tax, etc.

We would become something like a really big, really empty, really dark, and possibly really cold indoor farmers' market. Not a pretty picture. In all honesty, I would lock the doors. So would my competitor down the street (who doesn't even have six hours of backup power). So would everyone else in town, from the 7-11 to Wal-Mart.

This is not idle conjecture, by the way. Perhaps some electricity providers will be ready by the big day, but my local electric company began its remediation efforts earlier this year. I have little confidence that they will make it. The loss of electricity is a very real threat.

And that's just electricity. Even if electricity were to work, disruptions elsewhere could close me as well. Should the phones not work, we would not be able to transmit orders to our warehouse. Should transportation difficulties arise, we might be unable to re-stock even if we were able to place orders. Should there be civil unrest, well, I'm not going to place my life at risk to stop the spikey-hairs.

I would love to be the hero and keep my store open and feed everyone who needs food. I like selling food. But I can foresee many difficulties in achieving that. Quite frankly, at this point, such a task seems improbable.

We can live without The Gap. We can live without science fiction booksellers. But should my store, and my industry, have to lock its doors for an extended period of time, many will suffer. #

Finding Each Other in Hard Times

By Cynthia Beal

John Neal wrote:

Do you fear the economically deprived sections of our large cities? History has proven that these people are better equipped to survive hard times than the "upper" classes. In 1929 when the suicide rate on Wall Street soared, it didn't change at all in Harlem. Instead of fleeing from this sector of society, you should probably migrate toward it. This sector of society has, through necessity, preserved the skills you need to acquire in order to make it through hard times.

This insightful observation speaks to the edge of fear I sense in so many cities of half-strangers about to face the threat of Y2K together. For a quick view on the history he refers to, read Studs Terkel's "Hard Times."

We Americans live an average of seven years in a place; maybe even less today. We often don't know our neighbors very well— certainly, we've not grown up with them—and sometimes we're very suspicious about others' intents and purposes, since we don't have a life background in which to place each other.

Our friends and family are scattered around the world but we don't notice that as much, thanks to the telephone, electricity, gasoline, and air travel—all facilitated by computing technology. We depend upon our "network of connections" for our survival, in business and personal life, and so no wonder it's difficult for folks to imagine that such a thing as a series of Y2K glitches that gum up the works could even be allowed to happen.

In the poorer areas of town people stay longer, because they often can't afford to leave or, more importantly, they value the social capital of community more than the material capital of rising equity in a suburban home. And so, when truly hard times hit, these dense areas resonate with family, and neighbors, and people who aren't strangers to one another. Even if you've had hard times, you know each other—and real, bigger-than-the-neighborhood trouble mends fences quickly if people are allowed to work together.

The challeges Y2K presents to this community are, however, more difficult than ever before, because the infrastructure challenges of food, water, heat, fuel, waste removal, health care and social order are only partly addressed by clan resilience. Assuming that more policing is what these urban areas really need is doing a disservice to their greatest strengths. Continued disinformation to these communities only heightens the likely material stressors upon them, and it's here that I am most frustrated by the lack of attention to Y2K-impacts by our established communities-of-concern.

I also appreciated John Neal's statement because I am a small grocer in a downtown mid-urban setting who is trying to do many of the things Robert Mangus suggests with respect to staff and customers and key partners whom I trade with. It isn't easy, but it's the best next thing to do. [Reader: I am trying to get the Mangus suggestions referred to on my web site at www.co-intelligence.org. —Tom Atlee]

My grandmother was a grocer in Harlan County, Kentucky, during the Depression. She went out of business with her neighbors owing her $30,000 for food she gave away, on credit that was never repaid. Her store was the community cushion, her bank account the community deep pocket. My grandfather was in the coal mines, and worked with the United Mine Workers' strikes that resulted in a change for Appalachia. We can anticipate both recession/depressions and strikes (both worker and nation-based) related to Y2K, since the time is bringing both natural market correction and artificial market pressure.

Those were hard times. My grandmother would be one of the people blithely referred to by national "leaders" in current "expert" fiscal reports, one of that acceptable 5%-10% of affected small businesses that will fail, or whatever the statistic is by now. I suppose, as her grandaughter, it's only fitting that I be in these grocer's shoes today. And, like her, I do not find being in the "acceptable" group of those who fall through the cracks any more appealing than I have in the past.

But Granny also said there were always those who wouldn't help themselves, even in the Depression, sitting on the porch in the summer when they should have been growing and putting up food, and then begging in the winter when they were hungry, their children without clothes, school books or shoes.

Granny also said that anyone could have a small yard garden and feed themselves enough extra to make it feel like it was good, or at least enough. Something was better than nothing. She said the main thing you had to do was work, and that there was always plenty of work to do, and that the payment could be other than cash money, and anyone who said otherwise just couldn't see.

Although I'm a lover of the land, I am not recommending a flight to the hills, though I have, for over twenty years, been advocating an urban-rural partnership that keeps communities in touch with their interdependence on the strengths of both metropolitan and open-land values.

I call this sustainability. A huge body of current well-reasoned lore exists to support this, housed in the Sustainable Agriculture, Sustainable Development, Natural Step, the Human Potential, and Community Food Security movements, to name just a few.

These movements are replete with methodologies for communicating rapidly to lots of people, and working out effective strategies for change. In fact, one reason a number of the best ideas from these movements haven't been picked up by a lot of people, even though they make great sense, is that the inertia of the status quo has been impossible to overcome in small bites. With Y2K, this inertia will be temporarily upset, and there is a huge possibility for people to redirect lives and businesses and community goals opening up temporarily, and very soon.

I will not be leaving my downtown store because of Y2K. I'll be staying as put as I can afford to. I will not be leaving my rural rented farmstead unless the same thing happens. One foot in the country and one foot in the city. Each of us who works this way becomes a bridge for country and city to trade with each other, and there must be many more of us, independent, small-scale and vitally redundant, to heal the brittle infrastructure that embeds us. There's no money to be made here, but there's a living.

I guess I, too, join Leon Kappelman as an apologist for The Economy (whatever that is), a dynamic economy that makes room for as many different ways to approach Y2K, and any phenomena that affects value, as there are people to do the approaching.

Everything anyone does to heed and heal this problem will reverberate throughout the technologically dependent world. Any gift of time or thought we give that repairs damage, and communicates that fix freely to everyone else, is a gift that surpasses cash a thousandfold. A stitch in time...

The risk in actively raising our communities' awareness on Y2K (aside from diverting too much time to the larger civic arenas when we need to be taking care of our own backyards) is mostly a risk to ego; if we're successful enough in raising mitigative awareness so that no damage results anywhere in the world, we'll look like fools.

Norman Kurland of Computer Professionals for Social Responsibility said that our goal at this late date is to look as foolish as we possibly can on 1/1/2000; the last thing we should wish is to look sage and wise in an aftermath of expensive and damaging global nuisances and catastrophes. If we end up fools, friends, we've succeeded!

The more time we have to do this work of mitigation, the more equitable and pervasive the preparations can become, and the more politely we can make them. Because really, when you get down to it, aren't we simply doing the same thing we've always done—securing food, water, shelter, health, and a future for our children and the precious lives of this planet? Don't we always hope to discard the destructive and support the best, and don't we despair when we can't?

What's wonderfully different at this juncture is that, if we can get our poots in gear, the frame of Y2K has many of us looking to each other for the first time in recent history and asking, "Are you okay? Are you Y2K okay?" Not, "I'm okay, you're okay" but a true inquiry. "Are you REALLY okay?" Sure, it's motivated by self-interest, but even old Socrates himself points out that the larger one's idea of Self, the more deeply rewarding self-interest can become ("On Friendship," Versenyi's translation). [Frances Moore Lappe and Paul DuBois address this in their book, as well, "The Quickening of America." — T.A.]

And sure, we can continue to complain about the selfishness we see. We can pundit from the sidelines, and judge the people who are actually dealing with Y2K in the open, and sort them into camps, and denigrate or exult them as our personal preference dictates. We can exploit the scene for our own agendas of living—and in fact, will have to, because we've been charged with picking out what is most important and then preserving only that.

We can continuously rant on about the human frailties that have led us, largely unaware, to this pass, and the downsides of narrowed self-interest that funnel certain types of gain into certain types of pockets, but each moment spent complaining is a moment not spent fixing the problems or changing the world. We all have the same deadline to meet.

Attention is a currency today, and it will reap as it sows, with a bounty that can be shared by all of us. Thank you so much, all of you, for paying attention. #

Cynthia Beal is owner of The Red Barn Natural Grocery in Eugene, Ore., and operates the Medicinal Plant Conservancy in Lane County, Ore. For further information see Appendix A.

On Why We Need Y2K Lifeboats

BY REV. DACIA REID

May 3, 1998 Sermon
Universalist Unitarian Church of Brockton, Mass.

I must preface this sermon with the observation that it is a throwback to the early days of Unitarian preaching. Lengthy and dense! I always try to be well documented but this one's got 20-plus footnotes. I tried to find ways to make this topic into your average 15 minute sermon. I didn't like them. I felt that going shorter put you in the position of having to accept my assessment of the situation without any presentation of some of the currently available factual information.

I believe that you would rather make up your own minds than have me tell you what to think. I will tell you what I think towards the end of the sermon, but first let me offer you some of the basic Y2K information currently available. It is, I believe, food for much thought.

REMEMBERING AN OLD STORY

As I've become more and more engrossed in Y2K issues, one Bible story has come to mind on more than one occasion.

It is the story of Joseph (of Joseph's Technicolor Dreamcoat fame) as well as the Old Testament book of Genesis. In the story Joseph, who has been sold into slavery in Egypt, becomes known for his ability to interpret dreams. When the Pharaoh has difficulty getting a satisfactory interpretation of a particularly strange dream, he eventually hears of Joseph and sends for him. Joseph tells the Pharaoh that his dream of seven fat cows and seven thin cows means that lean times are coming and that he should use the current prosperous times to lay up stores against the coming time of famine. The Pharaoh accepts Joseph's interpretation of the dream and decides to follow its direction. Later in the story, only Egypt is prepared for the great famine that eventually comes.

Our culture is presently in the position of receiving a warning—in good times—that there could be serious trouble in the future and that we would be wise to prepare. Egypt not only survived the famine, it also helped others who were less prepared.

It is remarkable that the Pharaoh decided to believe his dream and go to the trouble and inconvenience of preparing for possible difficult times in the future. This story could help us decide how to respond to circumstances that are coming into view.

A NEWER STORY

But these are old stories. Perhaps we need to add something newer to guide our thinking. The analogy about the Year 2000 computer failure problem that works best for me was drawn by a man named Roleigh Martin, who compares our computer-driven technological infrastructure to the Titanic. We all know what happened to the Titanic. The fact that the Titanic sank was a big disappointment since it was a marvel of modern technology and was supposed to be unsinkable. The fact that the Titanic sank was not a disaster. The disaster of the Titanic was the incredible and unnecessary loss of life. It will be helpful to hold the Titanic analogy in mind while we examine the Year 2000 computer failure problem.

THE PROBLEM EXPLAINED

Y2K—The Year 2000 Computer Failure Problem

It's easy enough to explain and, massively difficult to correct.

The issue is that dates in most computers are represented by just two numbers—67, 84, 98, 99, etc. The problem is that when we reach the year 2000—or 00—that the computers, driven only by mathematical logic, will not know what to do. It will appear that time has gone backwards or started over. Most of us will not even have been born, let alone be old enough to receive Social Security benefits.

Understanding that 00 in this case means the arrival of the year 2000 is a simple and logical deduction for us human beings. For a computer, however, without new programming input, 00 is inexplicable and, depending on the particulars of each program, the computer will respond in a variety of unpredictable *and* always incorrect ways!

In the late 1950s and early '60s when computers were first coming into wide use in business and government applications, memory—computer memory—was hard to come by and very expensive. Companies could save $100,000 by having programmers use two digits instead of four to represent dates. Thus 1998 is generally notated as

'98—a simple shorthand solution, widely used by human beings and computers alike.

Bob Bemer, a 78-year-old resident of Dallas identifies himself as the grandfather of Cobol, the man who made it possible for programmers to use two-digit programming. He was a hero in the '60s. At that time businesses and programmers alike expected such rapid developments in technology that all their two-digit date solutions would be long gone, replaced by newer more powerful, more efficient equipment, long before the year 2000 every appeared. (#1)

Businesses and engineers in the 1960s at the dawn of our modern computing age correctly anticipated cheaper memory. They incorrectlyanticipated the 100% replacement of early technology and incorrectly presumed a switch to using four digit dates when memory finally got cheaper.

COMMON RESPONSES & ASSUMPTIONS ABOUT Y2K

No Big Deal—I don't even own a computer.

Perhaps you don't own a computer. But your bank does, your paycheck is computer generated, your health insurance data is computerized. That plane trip to Florida is computerized from scheduling, ticketing and baggage handling right through air traffic control. Your pharmacy and your doctor keep track of your medications by computer. Your tax refund or payment is processed by computer. Your grocery store orders its supplies via computers, and the truck and rail freight delivery of those groceries are scheduled by computers. Medicaid, Medicare and Social Security claims and benefits are processed by computer.

It's such a simple little problem—how can it possibly be such a big deal?!

Well, it's only, sort of, simple. And it's not little by any stretch of the imagination. It is estimated that one out of every 20 lines of program code is date sensitive. (#2) Bank Boston found that it had over 273 different programs and at least 50 million lines of code. (#3) The IRS has 80 mainframe computers, 1400 mini-computers and 130,000 PCs. They estimate that they have 85,000 programs, which need to be reviewed and fixed while the programs are simultaneously undergoing 800 changes to comply with new tax code. (#4)

At the one-out-of-every-20 rate, that means that Bay Bank must fix roughly 2,500,000 lines of code. (Note that the fixes are generally 4 to 8 lines of additional code.) Bank Boston started their Y2K project in 1994. They anticipate being ready to test their fixes sometime this year, which gives them a very necessary year to find and fix the fixes that didn't work, as well as the problems they missed or created with other fixes. (#3 & #4)

For the IRS, at the one-out-of-every-20 lines of code rate, there will be at least 3,500,000 lines of code to repair. They only started assessing the problem in 1997. Experts testifying to House and Senate committees claim that they can't possibly finish all the recoding, let alone any testing, before 1/1/2000. No time for testing is a sure recipe for trouble. (#5)

They'll get it fixed—they always (we always) find a way.

We've been using some of our computer systems for more than 40 years. Over that time we've been fixing them all along, adding on a patch here and there, as well as attaching and networking various systems as needed. These additions have been creative and efficient until now. As we confront Y2K, we face an incredible hodgepodge of programs—all using different methods of managing dates—all interacting with other programs in different ways.

Suddenly all those jury-rigged solutions patched onto older programs present a nightmare of undocumented, non-standard code— that defeats all possibility of any single effective fix. There is no magic, only tedious, repetitive, painstaking work. It's the kind of stuff we usually assign to our computers! But, because of the incredible variety—an extraordinary feat of customization—computers can do very little of this work. Instead, programmers with fairly high levels of skill must review and repair the code line by line.

Get those skills—and you've got a job.

Why don't we just . . .

Let's just repeat 1999 until we get it fixed. You know, 1999a, b, c, etc. Or let's go to a 99-day month and a 99-month year.

For a total of 9801 days in 1999. (If you're scheduled to retire in 2000, you're going to have to wait almost 27 more years to get to your retirement date on that calendar!)

Ingenious and somewhat practical by human standards, these ideas both would require more work to tell the computers what to do than the work of actually fixing our present Y2K problem. Both are strong testaments to the power of the human brain in comparison to the computer, and either solution would leave intact the same Y2K problem we currently face.

What has to be fixed?

Every business, every government agency, every town and city, every power plant, standard as well as nuclear, every sewage system and water treatment facility, every grocery story, every hospital, school and police department, virtually all aspects of our lives and culture are computerized.

Every computerized organization has to find, fix and test the Y2K problems in their computer systems. Fifty million lines of code is not an unusually large number—it's probably about average.

Statistically speaking...

Statistically there are at least 100,000 of the old main-frame computers still in use. They are the backbone—workhorses of government and industry. These are the ones that the '60s engineers and business leaders were so sure would be replaced long before now. Every one of them is programmed in either Cobol or Assembler— both languages that aren't even taught in our colleges anymore.

There are 300 million personal computers. The PC itself may or may not be Y2K compliant. Applications, particularly those customized to interact with the old mainframes, generally are not compliant.

Finally there are between 25 and 50 billion embedded chips. (#6)

So let's get cracking! What work is being done?

Two fixes in progress:

Medical Mutual of Ohio successfully processes 1 million claims a month.

Their Chief Information Officer began to research Y2K issues in 1995. He found that Medical Mutual of Ohio had 25,000 computer programs on 70 different operating systems in 36 locations across several states. Their 3,300 PCs and 800 other terminals were networked to each other and various mainframe computers via a hodgepodge of networks—mostly undocumented.

In 1996 the CIO went to the Board with his Y2K report of findings and concerns. The Board authorized $5 million. They hired a consulting firm and started planning how to accomplish all the necessary changes while continuing to run the company.

They began their "fix" work in 1997. One of the biggest issues was how to protect the corrected programs from contact with, and resulting contamination from, yet-to-be-repaired programs. Such contamination could undo thousands of hours of work.

In March of this year (1998) they reported that three of their 10 core clusters are completed. The other seven are well underway with completion expected in June of this year. Which leaves them with an ample 18 months for testing, which includes repairing undiscovered glitches. (#7)

Bank Boston tells a similar story—having started work in 1994. They have testified to Congress that they are satisfied that they are going to make it—but that they can't imagine how those just starting are ever going to manage compliance by 1/1/2000. They also raise the alarm about the need for their suppliers to be compliant—otherwise Bay Bank risks re-contaminating their carefully fixed code. (#8)

INTERCONNECTEDNESS:
THE SCOPE OF THE PROBLEM IS EVEN BIGGER THAN IT SEEMS

We Unitarian Universalist's talk about the Interconnected Web of Life of which we are a part. It's our 7th Principle, in which we are talking about creation, our planet, the world around us and all other forms of life.

There's another interconnected web—that also touches all of our lives. . . it's created by humans and it's technical.

Ecology conscious humans, rightly, raise many concerns about the well-being of our planet. Our sophisticated, technical, computer driven web, in the face of Y2K, is proving to be even more fragile and endangered than our planet. There are myriad ways that we rely on computers to interact behind the scenes. Our lives are computer orchestrated in virtually all areas from national security and air traffic control to catalog ordering and computerized auto repair diagnostics and parts inventory.

What Medical Mutual of Ohio and Bank Boston and every other task force assigned to Y2K are finding is that fixing their own code is not enough! If your customers and suppliers have not also fixed their code—you either won't be able to interface with them or their "dirty" code may corrupt your newly fixed code.

The extensiveness of our interactions between computers is impressive when we point with pride to our efficient economy, and mind-boggling when you consider it in the context of Y2K concerns.

LET'S CONSIDER A FARMER WITH GREEN BEANS TO SELL

The farmer sells into the market, when his crop is ready, via computer—his own or a buyer's. The buyer arranges pick-up and delivery with a trucking firm and sends notice of the purchase via computer. The buyer sells, via computer, to a processing center, which via computer, arranges pick-up and delivery. At the processing center—which is largely automated, the beans are spray-washed and boxed. The processing center, via computer, sells to a wholesale distributor which arranges transport via computer. The wholesaler sells the green beans, via computer, to a grocery chain, arranging delivery via computer. The grocery chain receives, via computer, the green bean requests from its various stores and arranges, via computer, for delivery to specific stores. The produce manager, via computer, schedules the department's employees for work. One of them checks the computerized inventory and task lists and puts the green beans out for sale. You or I come along, grab a plastic bag (conveniently available at the store due to another whole string of computerized transactions.) We fill the bag with as many green beans as we want to buy. And after selecting a number of other items—each available because of a myriad of computer interactions, we make our way to the checkout counter where a human being assists a computer in tallying up our bill, and the computer assists the human with making change which, thanks to computers, has become a largely lost art. If the green beans had been canned or frozen there would be several other computer interactions for processing the beans, and purchasing correct containers and labeling.

So, just in case you were one of those people who thought that Y2K wouldn't effect you, because you don't have or use computers, you might want to reconsider.

THE RIPPLE EFFECT

For many companies, the realization that simply fixing their own company's code may not be enough of a response to Y2K is a startling discovery. Fixing your own code only solves the problem if every other company with which they interact has also fixed their code. This Ripple Effect—that a problem in one company can expand outward to affect other companies—just like a stone tossed into a quiet pool of water, is giving business a powerful experience of an interconnected web. And at any given time there can and will be more than one set of ripples. (#9)

EMBEDDED CHIPS: A MAJOR COMPLICATION

You are, perhaps, coming to understand why we need to be concerned—100,000 mainframes & 300 million PCs represent a virtually unimaginable amount of code to fix. One observer speculates that, "The logistics for fixing this [Y2K] problem are more complex than preparations for World War II." (#10)

And this is still not the full scope of the problem. There is an enormous additional complication—embedded chips. Embedded chips are tiny microprocessors that are part of almost every modern device. They're called "firmware"—meaning that their programs are permanently loaded or burned in—unchangeable. They are almost as common as nuts and bolts and are treated the same way in terms of installation and documentation. They are just a convenient piece of equipment that facilitates a larger goal, upon which we've come to rely.

American Automotive manufacturers, Ford, Chrysler and GM, all started fairly early to work on their Y2K issues and expressed great confidence about the effectiveness of their preparations. They also got an early start on requiring compliance from their suppliers.

Then, last year, Chrysler shut down its Sterling Heights Assembly plant to test their fixes. They set all the clocks in the plant to 12/31/99. They expected to find some computer glitches—but they were really unprepared for what happened.

Chrysler Chairman, Robert Eaton, reported that nobody could get out of the plant because the security system absolutely shut down and wouldn't let anybody in or out of the buildings. And they couldn't have paid people because the time clock systems didn't work. (#11)

General Motors conducted similar experiments, and their CIO, Ralph Szygenda, stated that, "At each one of our factories there are catastrophic problems. Amazingly, enough machines on the factory floor are far more sensitive to incorrect dates than we ever anticipated. When we tested robotic devices for transition into the year 2000, for example, they just froze and stopped operating." (#12)

Virtually all of the problems Chrysler and GM discovered happened not because of problems in their newly corrected code. The problems happened because of embedded chips in nearly every piece of equipment in their factories. Chrysler as well as others doing "early" testing of Y2K fixes were shocked to discover such enormous, unexpected vulnerability.

BILLIONS OF CHIPS

There are 25 to 50 billion embedded chips in use worldwide. That's 4 to 8 chips per person. Experts estimate that somewhere between 1/10th of 1% to 2 or 3 % of these embedded chips will fail come 1/1/2000. (#13) That's a minimum of 50 million failures due

One writer compares the embedded chip problem to needing to treat every freckle on every human being, in its exact center, between now and Jan. 1, 2000.

to embedded chips, any one of which could shut down an entire assembly plant.

The challenge is that we don't know which ones will fail and they are everywhere. Thermostats, commercial, home and prison security systems, fire alarms, elevators, sprinkler systems, engine management, radar and navigation systems, communication networks, and medical equipment, including some pacemakers. (30) A single off-shore oil rig has 10,000 embedded chips, at least 1,000 of which are underwater. In many cases, an entire system can be stopped by the failure of even one of these chips.

Of course, the person living in a dirt floor shack in any Third World country is unlikely to have their share of embedded chips— meaning that those of us in first world countries will have more possible failures to contend with. Elevators and fire alarm systems are showing particularly high (80%) failure rates. (#14)

One writer compares the embedded chip problem to needing to treat every freckle on every human being, in its exact center, between now and 1/1/2000. (#15)

WE DON'T KNOW WHAT'S GOING TO HAPPEN!

It is clear that all of the Y2K problems cannot even be found, let alone fixed by 1/1/2000. So what's going to happen?! Nobody knows for sure. We live in "in betweeness." (A) There are plenty of people offering opinions. Here are a few reports to guide our assessment of potential difficulties.

The Hawaii Electric Company determined that without significant remediation their transmission network would crash, causing a major power outage and loss of all generating capacity. They're working on it. Many other utilities around the country have barely started. (#16) There are 9,000 electric utility plants in this country, very few of which have even begun to get ready for the Year 2000 rollover. (#17)

In Australia, when engineers simulated tests of the water storage facility at Coff's Harbour, they discovered that the system that regulates purification of the water would have dumped all the purification chemicals into the water on 1/1/2000, causing a mix toxic enough to kill the entire population of its supply area. (#18)

The Wall Street Journal on 4/30/98 had two front-page articles relating to Y2K. One quoting an executive at Paine Webber saying that the problem is being overblown by companies who want to make money on the fix. "Y2K will not derail corporate America, because the problem has been recognized and is being addressed." (#19) The second Wall Street Journal article was a survey of the use of computers in corporate America. It highlighted the frustration of many executives, who cite the fragility of overly complicated systems that never work properly, if at all, and noted that fully 42% of all corporate information technology projects are abandoned before completion. (#20)

Software is hard to build and hard to fix. If Y2K fixes are true to this norm, 42% of them are either not going to work or won't get done in the first place.

On April 30, 1998 the Brockton Enterprise ran an article from the Raleigh News & Observer (Raleigh, NC), that highlighted companies doing a lot of work on the Y2K problem. The article doesn't comment on the enormous size of the problem compared to the small size of the available workforce. It does say that Y2K work is expected to continue well into 2005. (#21)

We know that people are working on the problems. We know that they are going to work very hard, and . . . We don't know what's going to happen.

SOME THINGS THAT HAVE HAPPENED THUS FAR INCLUDE . . .

The President of the United States has created a Special Council on the Year 2000. The House and Senate have been holding hearings for a number of months. All government agencies are working to address the problem. Great Britain is devoting major energy to remediation as well as contingency planing led by Prime Minister, Tony Blair. (#22) And the Australian government has activated its emergency civil defense networks to prepare for problems. (#23)

On April 28, 1998 the United States Senate announced the creation of the new Senate Select Committee on the Year 2000 Technology Problem. Senator Bob Bennett of Utah said that their top worry is public utilities. "We have to make sure the power grid operates. Utilities, in addition to the all-essential electricity, include the processing and controlling of water purification plants."

Senator Bennett continued by saying, "Telecommunications— i.e. dial tone on 1/1/2000, come next; followed by transportation— particularly freight shipments, financial services, government services and general business services.

Senator Daniel Patrick Moynihan of New York, also on the new committee said, "I have no proof that the sun is about to rise on the apocalyptic millennium of which Chapter 20 of the Book of Revelation speaks. Yet it is becoming apparent to all of us that a once seemingly innocuous computer glitch relating to how computers recognize dates could wreak worldwide havoc. Today (4/28/98) there are 611 days remaining until Jan. 1, 2000—too late to lament, still time to act." (#24)

Y2K FANTASIES & REALITIES

Ignore it, deny it, fantasize about it, find someone to blame, find someone to sue, or prepare.

Personally I vote for preparation but first, let's consider a couple of Y2K fantasies.

In one of the Superman movies, Lois Lane dies when her car fills with dirt after falling into an earthquake-caused crevice in the road. Superman is so upset that he whooshes up into the atmosphere and turns the world backwards in time for several hours. Long enough to give him a second chance to rescue Lois. Maybe we could try something like that to get ourselves the time we need. Of course in the movie only Superman knows that time is changed . . . so we'd have to figure out how to alert ourselves earlier or it would all be a waste of energy.

Or maybe we could time-travel, a la *Back To The Future,* and convince those early programmers to use all four digits in the date. We might have to bring some of those early programmers into our future so they could see how important it is. In our movie this would be possible, and upon return, those programmers would be strong enough to get their bosses to resist the market forces demanding faster and cheaper computer use.

These fantasies are farfetched but about on par with the fantasy that everything will be fixed in time. Software programs are always late and once finished always have problems—bugs—that have to be worked out.

My husband says that in his 25 years of quality assurance work in the computer industry, he has only seen one software project completed on schedule. All the rest were late. In the world of software, late is rarely a big problem. It's normal for schedules to slip 6 to 12 months,with little consequence. Eventually the project gets done or replaced and everybody's happy.

The real problem with Y2K is that the deadline is unslippable! It isn't going to budge by even a minute, let alone a couple of months. This reality is part of the reason there is controversy around the Y2K repair efforts. Many of the folks attempting to manage the repair have not previously managed software projects. They are going about the business of setting up schedules like it's any other schedule. Programmers worldwide are overwhelmed, and those who take time to notice the trends in their industry are trying to warn people that no matter what the schedules say, the work cannot be done in the time available.

The time available (on 5/3/98) is just over 600 days. With barely 600 days left the likelihood that the whole world—or even just the United States—could pull off the successful correction of all 100,000 mainframes, 300 million PCs and 25 to 50 billion embedded chips is every bit as fantastic as turning back the clock.

But, if we could turn back the clock, I'd like to go back to 1970 when Cobol guru/grandfather Bob Bemer had gathered together 86 professional organizations, including the AMA, and submitted a proposal to President Nixon asking him to declare a National Year of the Computer. 1970 or '71 would have been a year during which all computer users nationwide (and by default, worldwide) would have concentrated on upgrading their date fields from 2 to 4 digits. President Nixon refused to sign the proposal, and it fell by the wayside. (#25)

GIVEN THE IMPOSSIBILITY OF ALL THESE FANTASY SCENARIOS, THE NEXT BEST OPTION IS PREPARATION

So let's find a way to think about Y2K that works.

Returning now, finally!, to the Titanic analogy: it seems farily straightforward to compare our computer-organized infrastructure to the "unsinkable" Titanic. (#26) The real disaster was that so many people died because of too few lifeboats, inappropriate use of what lifeboats there were, denial, inaction, and disbelief. I have a carpenter friend who says that he just can't believe that with all the materials on that ship and all the people on board that they couldn't have devised floatation platforms for virtually everyone in the two-plus hours it took that ship to sink. It would have been a lot better than having the band play on. One programmer compares fixing the Y2K problem to trying to replace all the rivets and metal fittings on the Titanic while it's rushing full steam ahead out at sea! (#27)

The best response for our largely non-programming population is to start building lifeboats.

Building Lifeboats

In 1961 the Department of Agriculture published a home and garden pamphlet titled, *Family Food Stockpile for Survival*. (#28) In it, the government observed that life is uncertain. Winter storms, spring floods, tornadoes, hurricanes and earthquakes are all possibilities within our United States. In addition there was the, then new, threat of nuclear war.

The government noted that even in an emergency, help cannot always reach people as quickly as they need assistance and advised each family to prepare themselves to be able to survive for 30 days without basic services and without government assistance. The pamphlet then lists the supplies that would be needed by a family of 4 to feed themselves for a month. It also includes suggestions about how much water storage is necessary.

I have no idea how many people actually followed these suggestions in the 1960s. I know that my family generally had extra food on hand but no stored water that I can recall and certainly no backyard bomb shelter.

I am of the opinion that the government should slightly revise and reissue this pamphlet.

The dangers of storms, floods, earthquake and nuclear war remain, and Y2K disruption of basic services looms ahead as a very real probability. You don't have to build a backyard shelter, but every family really ought to take steps to be able to sustain themselves for a week or two in the winter of 2000.

There is a pretty widespread range of predictions as to whether or not and how severely we may experience the arrival of Y2K. Some say it will be a non-event with business as usual. Others predict a total collapse of our infrastructure, and some faith groups are anticipating Armageddon.

How much you prepare will depend on your assessment of the likelihood of problems and how much help you think the government will be able to provide.

In January I talked about preparing for a three-hurricanes-in-a-row storm season. (B) George Goodman in the May-June issue of *Modern Maturity* talks about a "ten blizzards" winter. (#29) (C)

Whichever it is, three hurricanes, ten blizzards, a more major collapse or relatively minor, fairly temporary, disruption, the situation will not be isolated like a storm on the East Coast, a flood in the Midwest or an earthquake in California. Y2K will be everywhere—every town and city—all at the same time. If you think about this fact, it means that the usual government emergency responses will be stretched pretty thin!

I believe that the government will figure out how to respond, but that instead of the usual hours to a few days before they arrive on the scene it could be weeks! So why not be prepared?!?

The thing about lifeboats is that they are not individual. They are actually communal. A lifeboat generally holds a fair number of people and has to be launched with some help from people still on the ship.

So in addition to individual preparation it would be good to consider community preparation.

A church community could:

Find out what their town is doing in preparation for Y2K... electrical power, water treatment, sewage, police service, ambulance services, etc. Organize to educate their local government about Y2K concerns. Organize to copy essential papers—bank statements, mortgages, wills, etc.—notarize them and keep the copies at home and at the home of another church member. And groups of church members arrange for safe deposit boxes at various banks to hold the original documents. Maybe a member can become a notary to help with this process. Organize to make sure that elderly members have adequate plans for staying warm in the winter if the heat were to go off. Organize to make sure that all members who require special medications have an extra month of their prescription medicine available in their homes by Nov. '99. Learn about how to stay warm in the winter from members who are knowledgeable about winter camping. Devise a plan for checking in with each other and sharing news in the event of serious disruption of services.

These possibilities are going to be created by congregations.

We're used to weather reports! In fact we rely on them. We expect the weather bureau to provide timely and accurate information so that we can prepare for whatever the weather is going to offer. If it's a storm, we head to the store for water, candles, bread and milk. If it's a great day, we pack a picnic and head for the beach.

Either way we expect to be advised of the upcoming weather. I believe that the American people need to be advised of the unpredictability of Y2K. The government is reluctant because it doesn't want to alarm people. It's worried about a panic. With 600+ days to go we don't have to panic, but we could begin to prepare.

When each of us has access to adequate information we can come to our own conclusions about whether or not to prepare and to what degree.

My conclusions are that some level of preparation—being able to survive for a week to a month—is essential.

What if I'm wrong?

What if the experts are wrong . . .

1. I'll be relieved. I'd rather have this become a non-issue than a disaster.

2. The experts will also be relieved. . . Nobody really wants a major or even several minor disruptions to our economy and way of life.

What if you've decided to prepare and nothing happens?

In that event you will have a number of choices. You can save your supplies for the big hurricane or blizzard that will eventually make it necessary, or you can avoid the grocery store for a whole month, or you can make a nice donation to a food pantry.

Any of those scenarios seem to me to be far better than a failure of preparation.

We live "in betweenness." We don't know—we never really know—what's going to happen. We can turn away like Jonah, until circumstances force us to deal with the situation, or we can heed a dream, as Joseph and the Pharaoh did, and use the "fat" time in preparation for the lean years.

Our "fat" time isn't seven years; it's about 600 days. Six hundred days = 20 months = 85 weeks. If you started now, buying a little extra every time you go to the grocery store. . . a couple jugs of water every week and various non-perishable staples; powdered milk, rice, beans, M&M's—by Nov. 1999 you will have at least a month's worth of supplies.

I know that budgets vary. If yours is too tight to handle buying water and a little extra food every week, then remember that water is much more important than food. Human beings can survive much longer without food than without water.

So, at the very least, save all your milk jugs and juice bottles. As you empty a beverage container, rinse it out thoroughly and then fill it with water. Cap it tightly and store it away.

For myself, I'd prefer to make some basic preparations that I don't use rather than need a lifeboat and not have one, or enough, available. And, I really, Really, REALLY hope that each of you and this church community will choose to build a lifeboat or two as well.

Blessed Be, Amen! #

[See Appendix B for footnotes to this article.]

Since 1994 **Dacia Reid** has been minister of the Universalist Unitarian Church of Brockton in Brockton, Massachusetts. She became interested in the Year 2000 computer issue in the fall of 1996 and developed their UUY2K Project. She has been alarmed to notice that, despite all the costly remediation efforts, the single most efficient response to Y2K in our society to date is litigious! (Some experts speculate that the Year 2000 computer failures will result in a TRILLION dollars of litigation that will drag on for over a decade.)

Rev. Dacia Reid has been called a technophobe but she prefers to think of herself as a techno-realist.

The UUY2K Project is an effort to: 1. provide basic information about and links to the computer issues. 2. provide a survey of information regarding contingency planning. 3. explore theological and ethical issues, all within the context of Unitarian Universalism.

She holds a Master's of Divinity from Boston University School of Theology, Boston, MA and a Bachelors of Science in Education, Southwest Missouri State College, Springfield, MO.

She can be reached at RevDacia@uuy2k.org

Why community-based responses to the Year 2000 problem make more sense than individual survivalism

By Tom Atlee

There is a good chance that the Year 2000 problem will result in significant breakdowns in the social and economic support systems we've grown accustomed to. We will likely find it more difficult to get the basics of life, to say nothing of the luxuries. In many regions it is likely that people will only survive to the extent they have prepared for the possibility of hard times.

At this point it is not possible to predict how hard or how lightly any particular area will be hit. We may be able to predict this more confidently late in 1999. But by then there will be little time to make preparations — and any efforts to prepare will likely collide with the efforts of others, producing a more or less frantic mess. It seems wise to face the probability now that the Year 2000 problem will produce areas of significant hardship and even the possibility of widespread deprivation (of food, water, heat, etc.), death and social chaos. Prudence dictates that we make substantial preparations soon.

But what kind of preparations are most likely to succeed?

THE ROLE OF GOVERNMENT

We can always hope that our national and state governments will come to the rescue. Such faith is blind. Although most are doing something, none of them are doing enough for us to depend on and many of them are still doing little or nothing. Those who are active are primarily busy with their own computer systems; they are doing little to prepare for the impact of the Year 2000 crisis on the lives of ordinary people outside the realm of government services and regulations. Even if a government official or politician were to push ahead on our behalf, they would likely be hamstrung by fiscal and political constraints, and their ability to help will be further undermined in any location where the infrastructure (transportation, media, etc.) broke down. It may become very hard to get aid to areas most in need of it. In the worst case scenarios, governments themselves may collapse or become irrelevant.

Clearly, we can't count on government to save us. However, all levels of government could play essential and constructive roles in our collective survival through the Year 2000. We should actively push for them to make that a priority. In the meantime, we should also assume that we'll need to be much more self-reliant than usual. We might even demand that governments actively cultivate conditions in which widespread self-reliance can develop and succeed.

SELF-RELIANCE

But what kind of self-reliance am I talking about here? To what extent do we need individual and family self-reliance and to what extent do we need community self-reliance?

I will argue here that, dollar for dollar, hour for hour, ounce for ounce, building community self-reliance will yield a better return on our investments than building personal self-reliance. I will also describe ways in which community self-reliance involves mutual aid within and between communities.

SURVIVALIST AND COMMUNITY-BASED APPROACHES

Perhaps the most compelling argument for community-based approaches to preparing for the Year 2000 crisis is this: the more you and your neighbors invest your energy in a community response, the more synergy you can create. If four people who are each straining to move their own heavy tables get together, they can move all four tables quickly and efficiently. That's synergy. Together, a community is able to do more things that help the individuals in it, than those individuals can do by themselves. You waste less energy getting in each other's way and defending yourselves against each other. All of you together become greater than all of you individually. The more you each act to support a community response, the more powerful that response becomes, and thus more able to help each of you.

In contrast, the more you and your neighbors pursue a survivalist response—the more you invest in strategies that protect only you, your family, or those close to you—the more dysergy you create together, and the weaker your collective response becomes. Like tens of thousands of cars gridlocked on a highway or two kids fighting over a toy, everybody's efforts added together produce less progress than would be possible if they were alone. And we must face the fact that we are not alone; we are inescapably embedded in a society with millions of other people, all of whom face the same threat we do. The more survivalism there is going on in the society around us, the more our individual actions will start to undermine each other.

It can get quite messy. In a crisis where resources are scarce, differences between Haves and Have-Nots become vivid and disruptive. As those differences increase, so does jealousy, resentment and the sense of deprivation. Trust breaks down, and with it, social cohesion. The Haves invest more and more resources in defending themselves, while the Have-Nots invest more and more resources in stealing from or attacking the Haves.

To anyone viewing this from the outside, it would be clear that all those resources—all that time, attention, effort, and material resources invested in attack and protection—were being wasted. It would be like watching somebody who needed to open a door stand before it punching himself in the head with one hand while protecting his head with the other. Anyone watching this would wonder suspect madness. Why not use both hands to open the door? Similarly, why wouldn't the citizens of a threatened society apply their resources towards creating benefits of value to all of them, instead of fighting amongst themselves?

Perhaps only our outsider would notice, as well, that this struggle over resources was tearing apart The Commons—that shared environment of natural, economic, social and spiritual benefits and possibilities that normally sustains human communities. The participants in this intense survivalist game, obsessed with their own physical needs, would probably fail to notice that they and everyone else involved were systematically destroying important parts of themselves, their humanity, the quality of their lives and often the world around them. When everyone takes up the survivalist banner, everyone becomes a loser.

And so, paradoxically, in conditions of widespread breakdown, we find survivalism helping only a very few survive—and even then, usually helping them only for a short time. In a survivalist world, if you Have and most other people Don't Have, you become a target for everyone else's hunger, thirst, greed and resentment. If you are not willing to kill and steal, those who are willing to do so will take what you have. If you are willing to kill and steal, those who are more violent than you will destroy you or, if you are lucky, they will let you kill and steal for them in exchange for their support.

Most of us recoil at the very thought of such a dog-eat-dog existence. But we must face the fact that when people are starving and their community spirit is weak, such violent, Mafia-like power shakedowns are exactly what happen—and have happened throughout history, over and over again. They are happening today in impoverished city neighborhoods domestically and around the world. They are happening in Russia and Bosnia. They are an ugly but effective means of distributing resources. There is no reason that this sort of thing won't happen wherever the right conditions exist—that is, wherever there are scarcity, government breakdowns and weak community—exactly the conditions we could expect from a major Year 2000 crisis.

Survivalism can take different forms. The extreme individual survivalist heads for the hills with a stash of supplies, guns, and big dogs. A more mild individual survivalist keeps his stash at home and builds a higher, stronger, fence, or moves to a quiet small town in some tropical place (since the Year 2000 befalls us in the dead of winter). The collective survivalists move into gated communities with armed guards. The self-defeating dynamics of survivalism unfold for us no matter which variety we choose.

Survivalism is a tempting option because, although we may not have a lot of influence on the level of scarcity and or government breakdown in a Year 2000 crisis, we think we can control our own preparedness and destiny. I have tried to show that individual (or group)-against-the-world solutions are not as workable as they may at first appear. The alternative, of course, is community-building and mutual aid.

DON'T PEOPLE NATURALLY RALLY TO HELP EACH OTHER?

Some people suggest that pro-social community responses are natural and inevitable. They point to countless floods and earthquakes in which neighbors acted together spontaneously to meet community needs.

I would love to share that viewpoint. However, such events are different from widespread Year 2000 breakdowns in at least three very significant ways: 1) they are local, 2) they are temporary, 3) they happen with little or no warning, and 4) they are "acts of God." A Year 2000 breakdown may well be: 1) worldwide, 2) long-term, 3) largely foreseen and 4) created by humans, opening the door to blame and scapegoating. There may be no larger, healthy society upon which a traumatized community can call for help. As more people are threatened by deprivation, their loved ones will naturally rally more to meet their needs than those of their neighbors. In order to avoid fragmentation, the whole community's needs must be taken

The more equitable and resourceful a community we can create together, the less risk any one of us will end up facing.

into account ahead of time, by the whole community, and collective action taken to plan for contingencies. Such a collaborative community undertaking creates an environment in which pro-social responses can more easily surface and sustain themselves in a struggling population.

The fact is that both pro-social and survivalist tendencies are natural. But what we do now will make all the difference in the world regarding which natural tendency will predominate. We can have a lot of influence—starting right now—on the strength and self-reliance of our communities. If we support community responses, each of us becomes a co-creator of our community's survival and the general welfare. We receive benefits along with everyone else. The more equitable and resourceful a community we can create together, the less risk any one of us will end up facing.

WHAT IF EVERYBODY ACTS THE SAME WAY?

But before we leave the survivalist strategy for good, let us look at another of its glaring shortcomings—one so obvious that hardly anyone notices it: any survivalist approach will only be as successful if others don't do it. If everyone starts moving to the countryside and small towns, there will soon be no countryside or small towns left, and what little there is will be horrendously expensive—and will need to be heavily guarded—plus becoming increasingly unpleasant to live in. Another example: if everyone starts taking money out of the banks and stuffs it under mattresses, the banks will crash and robbers will soon realize that homes are becoming more lucrative targets than ever, ripe for the picking. Or if everyone starts buying up large stocks of batteries and preserved foods, the prices of these goods will skyrocket, making it harder for other people to stockpile their own stash and more likely that they will try to steal from the early stockpilers. If people are stockpiling guns and ammunition (and some are), this picture can turn very unpleasant, indeed, very rapidly.

In contrast, the more people act in a community-oriented way, the better the scene becomes for everybody. Any action by anyone on behalf of the community benefits everyone in the community. The more people join in teams to think and act together, the healthier the community becomes and the better the survival prospects for all involved. Some neighbors can prepare ways to collect rainwater while others are busy improving the community's capacity to provide accessible, low-tech medical care. While some are tending community gardens, others are teaching their neighbors how to grow food in their homes or to gather edibles from the landscape. While some are arranging for security or setting up generators in community facilities, others can be helping neighboring communities become secure as well, reducing the chance of inter-community conflict.

Businesses who are part of this community enterprise won't try to make a killing off of community needs, and communities can form purchasing blocks to bargain for good prices from other businesses. If banks and other financial institutions are threatened, communities can create local currencies to help all their citizens and businesses cope. (Note: This list is just to give you a taste of what I mean by "community approaches" and is not intended as a program for any particular community. More details about community approaches to the Year 2000 problem will be explored in subsequent articles on my web site and continue to be developed over the next year or so.)

The stockpiling of commodities and foods is a trickier question, because this issue needs to be dealt with on a regional or national basis. Networks of communities, working with state and national governments, could arrange for the production of key commodities and for the development of systems through which necessities could be shared equitably. Here the communities' role might be to pressure the higher levels of governance to serve communities, collectively, rather than trying to force into place centralized systems that may, in January 2000, fall apart. Equitableness among adjacent communities will be very important for social cohesion. Once we're into the year 2000, a spirit and practice of mutual aid among communities will be as vital as it is within communities.

LONG-TERM QUALITY OF LIFE

While all of us need to reasonably prepare ourselves, our families, and those close to us for the likely hardships of the Year 2000 crisis, our wisest efforts will be spent working with others in our local communities. In the process, we may even discover—as thousands of people already have—that such community activity is more meaningful and rewarding than the fragmented, pressurized lives we've been living. Perhaps we will decide, as we build back from the breakdowns of the Year 2000, that we are going to hold onto that close community we have created. Perhaps we'll use it to start building a better quality of life together than the old mass consumerism ever gave us.

If we end up realizing that real community is always healthier for us than big government, big business and big individualism, then the Year 2000 crisis will have been an unprecedented gift, not only to us, but to all the generations after us. They will inherit our wisdom that the community approach is a good idea — not just for surviving crises like the Year 2000, but for living truly rich and satisfying lives into a long, long future. #

QUOTES

The good we secure for ourselves is precarious and uncertain... until it is secured for all of us and incorporated into our common life.
— JANE ADDAMS

The survivalist approach is just not a practical approach.... You can't head for the hills because everybody else is going to be in the hills.... This is a communal problem that needs a communal approach.
— PETER DE JAGER, leading Y2K authority
In a discussion at the Center for Strategic and International Studies

My own personal strategy does not include heading for the hills; it involves trying to keep my community together, after I've ensured my own family is prepared to the best of my ability. To poorly paraphrase, "No man is an island." That's where I expect to be spending a majority of my own personal time during most of 1999.
— RICK COWLES
Expert on Y2K impact on utilities

Reweaving Community Resilience

We have been aiming to create systems that never go wrong rather than systems than respond well when things do go wrong, as they inevitably will.

BY ROBERT THEOBALD

Y2K is a reminder that our communities, and the broader systems in which they are embedded, have become dangerously brittle. The directions in which we need to move are no different, however, than those which have been proposed by future-oriented thinkers for years and decades.

This brief piece suggests a way in which communities can start to organize the work which will reweave community resilience. This can be valuable for all sorts of disruptions, ranging from economic recessions now emerging in many parts of the world, climatic instabilities which are growing more intense, and Y2K itself. I am personally convinced that we shall accomplish more if we see Y2K as a trigger for change rather than concentrating our efforts only on computer issues.

The steps which will work in each community will vary widely. Those living in the Southern Hemisphere of the tropics face significantly different issues than those who could face winter without heat and without the ability to grow food at this time of year. The common element, however, is the need for a structure which will divide up the tasks and permit significant activity to take place. Here is one model which emerged from work at the First Presbyterian Church in Spokane, WA. The catalyst for thought and action will inevitably vary from community to community.

The first step is to inform communities about the issues in a way which maximizes the possibility that people will see the benefits of working together. There are two primary dangers: one, that people will panic, and two, that they will move toward individual survivalist tactics. Spokane is planning a community awareness week very early in the autumn [of 1998]. This will be the first step of an education working group.

A sub-group will work to see how we can broaden communication channels. They will contact the media in town and see which of them are most open to understanding the scope of the emerging changes. They will then route the most important knowledge about developments to them. This will help provide an alternative framing for the news and break through the current emphasis on maximum economic growth and technological invention.

Another sub-group will aim to link community leaders. Spokane has a broad group of leaders from many parts of the society, but they are not effectively linked to each other. An effective program can only be developed within a network structure which keeps the whole community on board rather than serving the already privileged. Events will play out quite differently if communities see difficulties as unavoidable, like an ice storm, or if they see them as a catastrophe brought on by uncaring power structures.

The second challenge is to mobilize the technical skills available in the community. Everybody who has equipment which may be affected by the Y2K issue needs to be helped to recognize the issue and to have access to the technical resources required to resolve it. Two groups can be involved which would normally be left outside our thinking. First, there are many retired computer people whose knowledge is particularly relevant to many of the problems. Second, many younger people now in school and university could spend the next eighteen months working to resolve real problems rather than in classrooms.

The third challenge is how to prepare for disruptions. This issue raises two levels of problem. First, we do not know now, and may not ever know, how large the problems will be. The essential difficulty is not the specific breakdowns in equipment but the intricate interconnections between systems which can have cascading results. There need to be preparations at all levels from the individual, to the sub-neighborhood and neighborhood, to the community. The appropriate mix is yet to be discovered.

In 1996 I was invited to give a series of talks on Canadian radio. I entitled them Reworking Success. The thesis was that we would only prevent disaster if we changed our vision for the future. Y2K has moved up the timetable for learning this lesson. It has not changed the nature of the challenge. A group of us are now working to create a series of satellite television shows that will enable people to see the opportunities we now have and what leadership will be most effective. You can contact me for more information at theobald@iea.com.

Alternative Scenarios for Y2K

Will we break through to a new era of collaboration?

By Robert Theobald

Even the most radical scenarios for Y2K seem to assume that there will no fundamental discontinuities. This is perhaps most noticeable, and most startling, in the case of survivalist visions. The basic assumption on which they are based is that it will be necessary to get out of the cities because law and order will break down. And yet it also seems to be assumed that those who stock food and other necessities will be left in peace to enjoy them. In fact, those people who are prepared to be the most violent will simply seize the resources which others have prepared for them.

The hardest reality to convey at the current time is that the stability, and increasing wealth, that people in the rich world have enjoyed during this century will not be sustained. It may be climatic instability that breaks this trend. It may be the growing shortage of fossil fuels. It may be the failure of our social systems that have been undermined by current economic beliefs. It may be Y2K and the technological hubris of our time.

Successful continuation of the human journey requires the greatest transformation in thought and action that has ever occurred. We have seen shifts from hunting and gathering to agriculture, and from agriculture to industry. These both created significant shifts in behavior, but they were all along a single continuum: a belief that human beings could and should dominate each other and nature.

It is this belief which is now being challenged. Our new understandings of physical science, expressed in chaos and complexity theories, require us to relate to each other and ecological systems in radically different ways. The new scientific understandings are highly convergent with the core of all the world's religions, which propose that we should live on the basis of honesty, responsibility, humility, love and a respect for mystery.

We are faced with humanity's next "exam." There are three pos-

If we were to decide to change our course now...
it is still possible to limit the pain and suffering
in the world.

sible outcomes of the exam. One is that we shall try to avoid taking it at all. We shall continue to assume that the currently dominant ideas will continue to work into the future. We shall act as though maximum economic growth strategies and a commitment to international competitiveness should remain our core strategies. We shall continue to believe that technology holds the key to the solution of all problems.

We may be able to put off the day of reckoning through this approach although even this is not certain. I currently believe that the only way in which it is possible to avoid the worst consequences of the Y2K issue is to develop a global cooperative process. This would be designed to ensure that the most serious problems were dealt with wherever they were located throughout the globe. This approach is simply unthinkable in our current competitive universe. The chances of this happening are further decreased by the current legal culture which ensures that institutions cannot be open and honest for fear of incurring liabilities.

The longer we persist in our current directions, the worse the eventual collapse will be. If we were to decide to change our course now, and to recognize that our real crisis is a spiritual one, it is still possible to limit the pain and suffering in the world. The longer we persist in ignoring the evidence around us, the less we shall be able to shape the direction of the new society we so urgently need. The pattern of events in the old Soviet Union should be a harsh warning to us. Communism collapsed, and there was nothing ready as a substitute. Conditions are so bad that life expectation there has declined dramatically.

We have misinterpreted the meaning of the collapse of the Soviet Union. We have seen it as the triumph of capitalism over communism. We would do well to heed the meaning of Willis Harman's question: "If capitalism were collapsing, would we see the warning signs?" I believe that the evidence is all around us: we are confronted by signs of economic, social, moral and ecological crises.

Fortunately, an enormous amount of work has already been done to describe the systems which could replace those based on economic and technological emphases. Even more importantly, there is abundant evidence that people are ready to support change that moves toward a higher quality of life rather than an emphasis on more goods. Our challenge is to recognize that a new culture is already being born around us. I am amazed, and excited, by how many people are ready for new directions. We need to provide people with opportunities to engage in conversations about these issues so they can think through, and then act on, their emerging understandings. I am currently developing both audio and video tools to support these processes: these will hopefully be available broadly in the fall and winter of 1998 through various broadcast systems. #

Robert Theobald has been working on fundamental change issues for 40 years and was listed as one of the most influential living futurists in the *Encyclopaedia of the Future.* He can be reached at 202 East Rockwood Boulevard, Spokane, WA, 99202, USA or theobald@iea.com. His latest book is *Reworking Success.* Audiotapes suitable for broadcast are also available. Robert Theobald is making plans for dialogues about resilience.

Protecting Our Community from Year 2000 Computer Chaos

By Paul Glover

Normal life could continue beyond January 1, 2000. However, there's strong evidence that disturbed food and fuel supplies could bring us a colder, hungrier winter.

That's because our national economy is thoroughly dependent on computers to manufacture, transport and count everything. And many corporate and government computers have been trained to believe that year 2000 is 1900. Those that do will shut down or spread malfunction. (See www.y2knews.com and www.y2kinvestor.com/sites.htm)

While the national economy depends on computers, the local economy could, with genuine planning, carry us through serious disruptions of national supplies. Here's what could happen, and what communities can do to become secure. Some of these proposed solutions may seem extraordinary; they merely reflect potentially severe situations.

FUEL:

Without fuel, our food would not arrive at stores, water would not move to hydrants or homes, telephones would become silent, buildings would freeze, and cars would stop. When enough computers collapse, life will get very tough, because computers manage the extraction, refining, transport of and payment for fuels. They manage the manufacture of the precision tools needed for these processes. Assuming that our top priorities are to provide food, water and warmth, we can do several things:

TO KEEP WARM:

Our prime preparation (beyond weatherization) should be to superinsulate housing (starting with glazing), which reduces residential fuel consumption by up to 87%. Communities that do this can negotiate bulk purchases with local utilities, because utilities would need to add less generating capacity to serve such communities, thus avoiding the costs of new power plants.

Local energy co-ops could put dozens of people to work insulating, by paying them local HOUR money, issued as grants. [Paul Glover created Ithaca Hours in 1991. —J.L.] HOURS would be accepted by every landlord and merchant in the locality because the city, towns and county would agree to accept HOURS for property tax payments. These governments would then pay their employees partly with HOURS. This cycle would generally expand job creation, business stability, local money retention and tax collection.

Residents should be prepared for an extreme emergency also—a massive power failure—by organizing to reside in public and institutional buildings which are heated by onsite generators. Larger stockpiles of fuel should be laid in before Year 2000, to extend existing supplies. An inventory should be created of any well-insulated large buildings with generating capacity. Underground structures are models of superinsulation.

TO PROVIDE FOOD:

Since most of our food is cultivated, harvested, processed, packaged, transported and retailed by distant large corporations which depend on computer linkages, food supplies could become irregular. And prices could rise. If we want to be sure to eat, we should not depend on imported winter food. An estimated 80 acres of hydroponic (manure slurry) double-walled thermopane greenhousing could grow enough winter vegetables for 30,000 people. Buffalo, New York uses industrial wasteland for such purposes (NYT 3/3/98).

Survivalists are already stockpiling food, which is a reasonable thing to do. Yet they won't likely survive the hunger of fellow citizens smashing through their doors. And how long could personal supplies last if the whole nation staggers? To make sure everyone is fed, municipalities could create food storage facilities (granaries and root cellars) and contract with regional farms for part of harvests. These facilities could be operated by independent nonprofits, which could also contract with local grocers and sell direct at the Farmer's Market. This is simply an extension of Community-Supported Agriculture (CSA), which has already taken root in the U.S. Residential attached solar greenhouses (permitted by amended setback ordinances) could both capture more heat and produce food. Public support for regional farms is the best investment we can make for our children. Further conversion of topsoil into suburbs is an attack on future generations. We can expand farmland retention by right-to-farm laws, and by removing county taxes from active farms smaller

Were a full food crisis to overtake the nation,
local farms, community gardens and greenhouses,
aquaculture and urban orchards could keep us alive.

than 100 acres that market 50% of their harvest through local outlets.

Were a full food crisis to overtake the nation, local farms, community gardens and greenhouses, aquaculture and urban orchards could keep us alive. Cities should commence planting fruit trees and berry bushes.

TO PROVIDE WATER:

First, water districts should stockpile a year's supply of fuel, while sponsoring water conservation measures. Second, we can cut our need for household water in half by manufacturing waterless composting toilets (which are odorless and create safe topsoil), and by installing cisterns to catch rooftop rainwater. Sounds primitive? Consider the alternatives, with fuel shortage.

TO PROVIDE TRANSPORT:

Supply of cars and car parts is extensively computerized. Even if GM and Chrysler are ready for 2000, many essential component suppliers will not function beyond 2000. The fueling of cars, trucks, and snowplows also becomes problematic. Transit thus becomes imperative, to move people and goods efficiently.

More primary reliance can be placed on trollies for reduced long-term fuel cost. In most areas, railroad grades still exist which connect local and regional destinations along the most efficient routes.

Many crosstown trips could be conveniently accomplished with bicycles. To do this we'll need safe and separate bike lanes. Ithaca, New York, is fortunate to have Recycle Ithaca's Bicycles, which has given away over 1,000 bicycles, and has hundreds more in storage.

TO MAINTAIN HEALTH:

The physical and emotional stress of this disruption will challenge public health. Conventional medical care itself may be limited by shortages of food, fuel, medicines and money. We must reinforce locally-reliant emergency technologies during any crisis, within population centers. During times of greatest vulnerability to infection, your personal health becomes a public health issue.

The Ithaca Health Fund (www.lightlink.com/healthfund) and HOURS have connected practitioners and clients via local currency. We intend to start a nonprofit dental clinic and Wellness Center.

TO PROVIDE HOUSEHOLD SUPPLIES:
Many tons of perfectly reuseable clothes and furniture are buried in landfills yearly. Thousands of students throw away computers, top brand clothes, furniture and fresh unopened foods when they leave town. Ithaca's Student Recycling Project has already recaptured a fraction of these goods for resale at garage sale prices. Their model can expand with a large storage facility, truck fleet, and retail outlet. They could gradually replace department stores.

FINANCE:
Everyone expects to get paid. Millions of tasks by billions of workers combine to make products which keep us alive. Computers handle a large part of the credit transfers, which entitle workers to obtain food and fuel when it is available.

However, many banks are expected to scramble accounts; some ATMs have already misfired; some credit cards have jammed. Even large U.S. banks and corporations which manage to prepare for 2000 can expect to be dragged into confusion by the noncompliant banks of the Third World, and by noncompliant small suppliers. The stock market will likely reflect this chaos: 83% of U.S. Y2K project managers expect the Dow Jones to fall by at least 20% (Y2K Wire 5/15/98).

TO SUSTAIN TRADE:
When we are forced to produce and trade locally without stable dollars, we will need to expand the supply of local money. HOUR money directly reflects the value of labor (www.lightlink.com/ithacahours), therefore we can measure local effort without depending on the unpredictable swings in global dollar markets. To trade HOURS independent of dollar prices, communities need to create a local catalog of HOUR values. We could convene a community congress to recommend new HOUR prices for labor and goods, while allowing everyone to negotiate HOUR values independently.

The disruption of the macroeconomy might change existing labor priorities. During a severe crisis, essential survival skills, especially physical skills, become more valuable. Thus, one hour of farm work producing food might be more highly paid than one hour of legal advice.

In the worst case, without reliable dollars, HOURS will function to the extent that localities become self-reliant in the production of necessary goods, and to the extent communities are prepared to properly issue their own HOURS and trade them with one another.

Likelier, less extreme yet serious disturbances would permit us to expand the HOUR supply more gradually. In either case, we'd be prudent to back HOUR issuance with fundamentals like landholdings, local natural gas drilling rights (by eminent domain), shares in local harvests, etc. This would enable us to readjust the HOUR supply (by redemption) were the dollar supply to regain credibility.

Confidence in the expanded HOUR supply could also be secured by local banks that want to contribute to the solvency of the local economy, by backing HOURS with donations of rental and idle rural landholdings. This would permit the issuance of larger HOUR loans at zero percent interest, to jump-start a damaged economy. As priorities, farmers could receive HOUR loans to hire laborers, and essential public works could be maintained.

We can maximize local production for local needs by creating an import replacement system, which inventories and connects regional raw materials, skills and markets.

COMMUNICATIONS:

At the first signs of malfunction, residents will start calling for help. If computers and telephones don't work, we'll turn to radio and TV for emergency information. If these media are down too, we'll resort to speaking with neighbors. To replace panic with coordinated action, we'll need to prepare independent communication links for dispatching emergency vehicles, for distributing emergency supplies, and for directing people to help. Here again, with fuel limits restricting private car use, bicycles and runners can serve to deliver messages.

If all the above sounds medieval, remember that humans lived very reasonably here for thousands of years without electricity or computers. Throughout the nation there are model housing developments which showcase comfortable housing with little or no electric use.

Typically, during any serious economic crisis, demand rises for redistribution of wealth from the rich to the poor, by legislation, food riots, and revolutions. If it becomes terribly difficult to be poor, then it will become inconvenient to be rich. To ensure an orderly transition that respects all persons and basic property, rather than risking violent upheaval, citizens can work together to bring us all through intact. With civic planning, we can have good lives after computers. Maybe even better ones. #

Paul Glover is founder of Citizen Planners of Los Angeles (1983). He is author of "Where Does Ithaca's Food Come From" (1987) and "Ithaca Power" (detailing Ithaca's fuel supply, 1988), and holds a degree in City Management. His Hometown Money Starter Kit and video are available for $40 from HOUR Town, Box 6578, Ithaca, NY 14851. Paul Glover, Ithaca HOURS, (607) 272-4330, http://www.lightlink.com/ithacahours, Box 6578, Ithaca, NY 14851, Ithaca Health Fund, Box 362, Ithaca, NY 14851, http://www.lightlink.com/healthfund.

What One Town Can Do

BY JIM LORD

IN MAY 1998 MEDFORD, Oregon, was the site of a remarkable community event. More than seven hundred people gathered together over a two-day period to learn how to protect their families and communities from the effects of the Year 2000 computer crisis. It was the first such large event held in the United States.

Eight hours of meetings and seminar sessions were offered to the public. An initial two-hour session was conducted at City Hall where an overview of Y2K was presented to city officials from Medford and several nearby communities. During this meeting, the nature of Y2K was explained and the primary risks of the crisis were explained. That evening, the same presentation was offered to the public and was followed by a lively and highly informative question and answer opportunity.

The following day, a Saturday, the morning session was devoted to individual preparedness topics. This presentation laid out a series of common-sense, practical steps that can be taken by individuals and families to prepare for possible disruptions in such critical goods and services as food, water, energy and medical supplies and services. Significant attention was also paid to methods for making financial preparations in the event of interruptions in the banking and other financial systems.

The final session on Saturday afternoon was devoted to community preparedness issues. Defining the extent of the problem and its possible impact on community infrastructure was particularly useful to the audience. This topic included an examination of the possible exposure of utilities such as water, electricity and sewage/trash removal systems, and such public services as police, firefighting, ambulance, medical services, senior care facilities, public education and so on. Community activism and organizational techniques were also discussed.

The startling attendance at these sessions indicated the high level

The New Age mystic and Joe Six Pack set aside their differences. For a day and a half, it was a magical manifestation of community togetherness.

of community concern about the Year 2000 problem. This impression was confirmed during several lengthy question and answer sessions during which the audience revealed the nature and extent of their concerns. Simply put, they were worried about the basic stuff of life. They wanted to know if the Year 2000 crisis might disrupt the availability of everyday necessities such as electricity, food, water and medical treatment. There was considerable anxiety that the government might be unable to provide critical services such as Social Security, Air Traffic Control and even military protection.

These high attendance numbers caught the local press by surprise. The seminar did receive excellent coverage before the fact by the local newspaper (two stories, including a front pager) and by the local broadcast media (four interviews). There was no press coverage, however, at the three large seminar sessions.

Some local political leaders were also caught unawares. The small city hall meeting in Medford saw representation from Medford, Ashland, Grants Pass, Butte Falls and Jackson County. Senator Smith (R-OR) sent a representative as well. As with the press, however, few, if any of these leaders were present at the larger seminar sessions. Nonetheless, those who did support the event are to be commended because Medford, and the surrounding area, will soon be acclaimed as the first community in the nation with the vision to host a Y2K preparedness event at its city hall.

The most surprising aspect of the Medford meetings was the broad diversity of the attendees. All political and religious persuasions seemed to be there. Young, Generation X working couples and Social Security recipients sat side by side in the audience. Environmental activists rubbed elbows with blue-collar workers. Christians and libertarians joined in serious conversation. The New Age mystic and Joe Six Pack set aside their differences. For a day and a half, it was a magical manifestation of community togetherness. Political leaders across the country should take note of what took place in Medford. A powerful coalition for good is standing ready to take on the "Millennial Bug."

What impressed us the most, however, was the remarkable impact one concerned individual could have in a community. The Medford event was organized by Will Reishman, a local investment counselor who simply cares about his neighbors. Under the sponsorship of Icare, Inc. a charitable public service organization, he singlehandedly willed the entire event into being. All expenses were defrayed through donation and all were invited to attend without charge.

The Medford Y2K Community Preparedness Seminar reminds us of these two simple messages: that people do still care, and a single person can still make a huge difference.

The Year 2000 computing crisis poses a frightening threat to almost every aspect of our way of life. Some believe it should be confronted with a remote cabin, a pile of dried food, a big dog, and a shotgun. This strategy, although perhaps rational on an individual basis, is unworkable for society as a whole.

Medford shows us why it is unnecessary.

Contemplation of Jan. 1, 2000 can easily cause feelings of hopelessness to creep into one's thoughts. It's not at all difficult to convince yourself that nothing can be done, that government isn't going to make it, that the world as we know it is going to come to an end.

The best antidote for these feelings of despair is to take positive action. Get a community group organized. Talk to your religious leader or a local charitable organization. Take advantage of the existing social support mechanisms in your community. The churches, in particular, are well suited to this task.

Also, get educated—information is your most powerful tool. The Internet is the critical source of up-to-date information, although a number of books are starting to come onto the market. Think about what the community impact of Y2K might be. Find out what is happening in Washington and in state and local government. At the same time, stop waiting for government to take care of this problem for you. Y2K is not the government's problem; it is yours. The solution is yours as well. What happened in Medford was not a fluke; it was just the first of many thousands of similar efforts that will take place across the country.

All it took in Medford was a single person who cared. #

[As this book went to press, a Southern Oregon Y2K Summit was being held in Medford, August 6, 1998, hosted by the Rogue Valley Y2K Task Force, and U.S. Senator Gordon H. Smith, member of the Senate Special Committee on the Year 2000 Technology Problem. —J.L.]

Jim Lord is a retired naval officer with 24 years active service, including a tour as the electronics maintenance officer on an aircraft carrier. He earned a degree in Business, graduating with honors from the Naval Postgraduate School in Monterey, California.

Following his military career, Mr. Lord was involved in shipbuilding, communication systems design, satellite systems, software engineering, training and marketing. This experience included nine years in the software industry.

Mr. Lord is the author of *A Survival Guide For The Year 2000 Problem,* a practical, 200-page, consumer's guide to preparation for the Year 2000 Computer Crisis. It describes the effects of Y2K on virtually all aspects of society and the economy. Particular emphasis is paid to government at all levels, employment, the financial sphere, and public services. Specific and detailed guidance is provided on how to protect yourself, your family, your assets, your job, your vital private data, and your personal safety from the greatest technical blunder in history.

He is also the publisher of *Jim Lord's Year 2000 Survival News-letter,* which provides continuing updates on the progress of the Year 2000 Crisis. This bimonthly publication closely tracks the status of government and industry efforts to repair critical computer systems. (To order, call J. Marion Publishing, toll free at 1-888-Y2K-2555.) Additional information can be found on the Internet: www.SurviveY2K.com.

Mr. Lord is also available nationally for speaking engagements. He resides in Davidsonville, Maryland.

Your Unique Role in Addressing Y2K

A personal checklist

By Tom Atlee

The Year 2000 crisis came about because of the actions and interconnections of computers and technological systems. The Year 2000 problem will be dealt with by the actions and interconnections of people with each other and with the natural world.

Now is a good time to realize your unique role in the world, and take the reins. Now is a powerful time to wake up to your unique capabilities and connections, to take responsibility for them, and to use them to make a difference in the life of your community and the fate of your culture. Y2K has created the right time to do this — individually and together with your fellows.

There's a lot you can do. There's no need to ask rhetorically, helplessly, "What can one person do?" Now is the time to ask that question for real. Ask it to find real answers that are right for you. Then take action, however small. The hardest part is doing one thing, the first thing. Once you've taken one action, you'll have begun your journey into your full power in this world. You'll know more how to go forward. Imagine you are one of millions doing this—because you are.

At the end of that journey together, we'll have a very different world. If we all do our part, it may just be the world we've always wanted.

If you are a professional

• Talk to your professional colleagues about Y2K. Write articles for professional publications. Run workshops and breakout sessions at professional conferences. Communicate with your colleagues through professional networks, listservs, etc.

Work out how your profession can be of service. For example:

• Engineers can help address infrastructure problems or promote sustainable technology.

• Medical professionals can ensure that basic health care services are available post-Y2K, and that public health and sanitation needs are prepared for. If medical equipment and modern drugs may be unavailable, low-tech approaches should be promoted, such as prevention, herbalism, and community health volunteerism.

• Educators can develop Y2K- and community-preparedness-related curricula (for both youth and adult education), help make school spaces available for community preparedness activities, engage the creative energy of children in community preparedness (they are often the best way to involve parents), and engage academics and graduate students in needed research (such as clarifying what enhances or undermines community resilience and pro-social responses to catastrophe).

• Mental health workers can help people work through their emotional responses to Y2K and set up emergency hotlines for people in crisis.

• Journalists can research and publish stories of successful community preparedness activities and dramatic human interest stories that empower readers to respond creatively to this crisis.

• Activists can work out how Y2K relates to their traditional issues, and do their activism in ways that enhance the ability of communities to respond.

• Spiritual leaders can call their spiritual communities into preparedness, service and spiritual growth.

• Politicans and civil service workers can find out how prepared their agency or level of government is for the year 2000, and urge those in charge to look beyond the readiness of their computer systems to the preparedness of the communities they are responsible for—especially vital infrastructure like food, water and sewage.

• You get the idea. Now think about your profession. If you have trouble thinking of what your profession can do to help, contact us at cii@igc.apc.org. We'll work on it and post the results. If you send us reports on what you're doing in your profession, we'll summarize them.

If you know anyone who is a professional, talk with her about Y2K and encourage her to do the type of reflection and activity described above. This will greatly magnify your impact on how this enormous event unfolds.

Make a list of other people you know, and contact them.
• By yourself, consider all your friends and family. Think about how to talk with them about Y2K. Decide who you are going to contact this week, then do it. Next week pick another few, and talk to them. Add to your list as you go along. Encourage them to do the same with their friends. Refer them to this site or give them printouts of your favorite articles. Help them think about what their own response will be.

• With a group of friends, neighbors or Y2K-concerned fellow citizens, brainstorm who you each know who might be able to make a significant difference in how the Y2K situation unfolds. (A group of six of us came up with over 50 significant individuals, organizations, agencies, media, networks, etc., that we had personal connections with. One person's connections would remind someone else of another person. That's why it's good to do this in a group.) Then figure out who can contact whom when, and get started.

Make a list of the groups and organizations you are connected to—churches or temples, community groups, special interest organizations, clubs, activity groups, political parties, and so on. Start with any that have particular power in your community or country, or in which you hold a position of power or respect. Look at their reason for existence and how Y2K relates to that. Choose who to communicate to, and how, and then do it. Then move on to other groups. It may make sense for you to create a small group within certain organizations to promote their involvement in Y2K. Don't forget your favorite neighborhood stores, libraries, etc. You can help them prepare using the Small Business Owners Year 2000 Readiness Checklist.

Make a list of at least ten government officials, politicians or agencies who are supposed to be serving you. If you do this with friends or associates, you can each pick one or two to write (or, better yet, call), discuss what you will say to them, and then later share with each other what happened when you did that. If you work together on this, you will find that what you should do next becomes clear as you go along. This approach is especially effective with national or state officials at all times—and with local officials up to a point. If one local official receives dozens of calls from Y2K-concerned citizens each day, it can interfere with her work, so be sensitive to her needs.

It matters less what you do together than that you build good relationships.

Make a list of media that you use —TV, radio, newspapers, magazines—both local and national. If you are in a group, divide up the list so that each of you is tracking the Y2K coverage of at least one of them. If they don't cover Y2K at all, ask them why. If they cover Y2K but don't cover community preparedness issues, or aren't covering Y2K in a way that empowers the community, insist that they correct their coverage. Use the information and links on this site to become knowledgeable, powerful consumers of Y2K media information, on behalf of your whole community. If you are ambitious, call in to talk shows—or begin to build a personal relationship with a particular reporter or columnist, and find out how you can help him cover Y2K better. Always validate good coverage; write reporters and tell them how much you appreciate it. An often-overlooked source of information in your community is your local library. Talk to librarians about Y2K resources that are available online, and ask if you can help them develop any other information resources. Use library spaces for Y2K meetings.

Connect with your neighbors. Realize that if there is a major collapse of infrastructure, the people you are going to be dealing with are your neighbors. There may be no media, no internet, no phones, no stores, no gas for your car... "Nobody here but just us chickens," as the saying goes. At that point, neither you nor your neighbors will be going very far from your neighborhood, nor will you have anyone else to talk to or work with. If you don't already know the people living around you, now is a very good time to have some street parties, share dinners, do neighborhood yard sales, get involved in neighborhood associations, start a neighborhood newsletter, join a crime watch or disaster preparedness group, or otherwise involve yourself with your neighbors, even if it is just to say hello and chat for a minute as you walk by. It matters less what you do together than that you build good relationships. As the months go on, you'll be able to align your conversations and activities increasingly to the demands of Y2K, since it will probably become a growing concern for everyone. Encourage your neighbors to do the things mentioned in this article, and encourage your friends, relatives and associates to get to know their neighbors. Then, whatever happens, our communities will be fully alive again!

Think about how to help with your unique abilities.
• Do you like to take care of children? You could offer to take care of children at Y2K meetings.
• Do you do artwork or promotion? You could design fliers or create murals and posters.
• Do you design web sites? You can offer your services for a local (or national) web site on Y2K.
• Do you like gardening? Start a community garden for your neighborhood (especially with kids!).
• Are you a fix-it person? Start fixing up old broken bicycles. They'll be needed!
• Were you alive 60 years ago? Then you probably know how to do many things that younger people cannot do because they're so dependent on technology. Prepare to teach the practical skills you know—sewing, herbal medicine, entertaining children without TV, etc.
• If you have trouble thinking of how to use an ability you have, contact us at cii@igc.apc.org. We'll work on it and post the results online. If you send us reports about how you're using capabilities we haven't yet listed, we'll summarize them.

Think about your investments. Your money could—
• Help develop sustainable technology industries (solar power, water purification systems, etc.),
• Support businesses that support their communities or operate ecologically, or
• Further the projects of community development banks.

You can also become a "social investor," investing your money in activities like the Co-Intelligence Institute, where the return isn't more money but a better society and greater collective security for your community and your children. If you think Y2K is going to be really serious, take a serious look at what money means in this new context. Using it now to make the world or your community better may produce enormous returns in aliveness and meaning, where trying to figure out how to protect it in a ferociously collapsing society may drain away aliveness and meaning. Notice how you feel. Move into a relationship with money that is most alive for you. It will probably be the one that most nurtures the health of our shared world.

Strengthen your connection to nature.

Come home to nature: you are already connected to nature, even if you are locked in a prison cell. The atmosphere is nature. The bugs are nature. The rain and the sun are nature. You can always become more conscious of and responsive to the way you are embedded in nature, and the role you are playing in it. Are you participating in ways that enhance the aliveness and health of the natural world in which you live? Can you learn more about it? (See bioregionalism and permaculture for some ideas about this.)

Go out into nature: Hike, bike or camp in less inhabited areas. Familiarize yourself with the life that lives there. Sense its power, its wisdom (hard won through billions of years of trial and error), and its right to life and a place in the world comparable—at least!—to your own.

Co-create with nature: Garden. Compost. Plant a tree. Protect a forest or wetland. Walk. Do what you can to re-use water (greywater, rainwater, etc.) instead of sending it down pipes into the ocean. Do what you can to protect the air.

The industrial/economic infrastructure we've built around us makes us feel like we are outside of nature. We're not. It makes us feel like we don't need nature. We do. It makes us feel like we can abuse nature as long as we like and get away with it. We can't. Do what you can to make friends with the most powerful, all-pervading reality on earth, to become knowledgeable about its needs and demands, to become a partner in supporting its well-being so that it can support yours. It is vastly capable of supporting human culture, but it won't tolerate abuse. It demands respect.

Without our infrastructure, we'll have nothing but nature and each other to work with. Actually, we've never had anything else to work with. If the Y2K threat to our infrastructure teaches us this one lesson, it will all have been worth it. If we don't learn this lesson now, nature will give us an even harder lesson. Now is the time to get it right. #

Keeping Sane in Tumultuous Times

BY MARILYN TRAIL

In the spring of 1998 my Mother died, my husband developed malignant tumors along his spine and my daughter came down with typhoid fever in Mexico City. As I emerged from the fog of grief, fear and coping, I began hearing some information that raised the hair on the back of my neck. I heard futurist Robert Theobald speak at a Spokane civic forum about the hazards of consumerism, the new human behavior of preferring more stuff to more leisure, and the possible technology glitches caused by using two-digit-year identifiers.

I immediately understood Y2K. In the '60s I had written computer programs for the Army Corps of Engineers, mathematical models for researching the Columbia River Basin network of dams. The rainfall data were coded with two-digit dates.

As the implications of this information sunk in, I went through the emotions of shock, despair, then acceptance. Although my work was always theoretical, I saw that short-sighted "real time" programming, using two digit year coding, could indeed wreak havoc. I wondered about solutions and all the changes that had transpired since I changed professions in the '70s. (See how we do this! I should say 1970s!) The socially helpful concept of thinking of the effects of our behaviors on the next seven generations was not even a whisper in the hallways of the Army Corps of Engineers. Everyone was caught up in the promise of this exciting new technology. Because memory banks were small, minimizing data was vital. Or so we thought.

CONVERGING PROPHECIES

As I sat recently with this prospect, I remembered things I had learned in recent decades. I began pulling together strands from the past, coupled with new information, until a pattern began to form. How odd that so many prophecies from disparate cultures all indicated a major transformation around the time-wall of the year 2000. Could it be that the Y2K phenomenon was part of a greater pulse?

I dusted off an old copy of "The Mayan Factor" by Jose Argulles. (Bear and Co., Santa Fe, NM, 1987.) Certain chapters stood out: "Technology and Transformation" and "The Coming of the Solar Age." The two decades from 1992 to 2012 mark the end of a 26,000-year Mayan calendar. The emergence of *homo sapiens* is said to represent a stage in the evolution of our "star." We are now at the climax of our particular species, the Mayans predicted, coming out of the dark ages of the 20th century, into the light. We are remembering as a species that we are to partner with the intelligence of the sun. The avatars of Christ, Buddha and Quetzalcoatl kept alive the collective memory of our solar heritage. What does this mean?

In the chapter "Blueprint to the Year 2000" from *Black Dawn, Bright Day* by Sun Bear with Wabun Wind (Sun Bear Publishing, Spokane, WA, 1990), many natural cataclysmic changes are predicted, including earthquakes, hurricanes and volcanic eruptions, as well as disease and a breakdown of technology, political and social order.

Hopi Native American shamans, Australian Aborigines and many other humans living lightly on the land have similar predictions for changes on the earth and in our humanity. The common theme seems to be that the earth will change; we can't control it; we need to work with Mother Nature.

In April I visited my daughter in Mexico City, where the air was foul with smoke from many forest fires and volcanic eruptions. By the next month the smoke had spread from Monterrey, Mexico, to as far north as Ohio.

Thoughts, memories, useful creative images arise in my consciousness, and an old gospel hymn stirs me:

Sowin' on the mountain, reapin' in the valley...
God gave Noah the rainbow sign.

Won't be water, there's fire next time...
God gave Noah the rainbow sign.

Where you gonna run to, when the world's on fire...
God gave Noah the rainbow sign.

Sowin' on the mountain, reapin' in the valley...
God gave Noah the rainbow sign.

Another thread in my weaving of an integrated understanding of these many predictions was my work with the sufis. When I lived on

Bainbridge Island, Wash., I spent many years studying the works of the ancient eastern poet Rumi with a group of kind, intelligent people. I learned to respect all work (Ghandi had this same concept), and to love nature deeply. While attending a sufi retreat in Atlanta in 1986, we were told to buy some land, develop gardens for root vegetables especially, have a good source of water, and raise goats and chickens. *The times, they are a changin'.*

In my e-mail these days I receive invitations for global prayer, emphasizing that a critical mass of humans praying at the same time could alter the outcome of peace negotiations, or even the prophesied earth changes. With my left-brain scientific bent, how am I to integrate and be discerning? And as a social psychologist, how can I help foster an environment in my own city, Spokane, which will promote thriving and discourage panic and paranoia?

There are certain bedrock concepts which have always served humanity and which can serve us now. This is the emotional survival kit I have put together for myself:

Don't just do something, sit there. This reminds me to empty my mind, meditate and await the unfolding of wisdom.

Make peace with death. We all will die. Our purpose is to love each other, to live well, not necessarily long. Before deciding to live in an armed camp, for survival's sake, consider how that will feel. Hoarding will invite crime and violence.

Trust. We are here now for a reason. We have purpose. Tune into inner stirrings, trust and go with them.

Hone your sense of humor! The law of levity is stronger than the law of gravity. Laughing brings more oxygen into the body. Do it often.

Grieve. Crying is healing, and loss is painful. Move through it.

Recognize fear and feel it. Find comfort in a hug, a blanket, talking to a friend, taking a bath.

When you are angry, wait. Count to ten, or higher. Take a walk. Learn negotiation skills. "Don't sweat the small stuff, and it is all small stuff."

Pray. Ask for help from your Higher Power.

Start or continue to get to know your neighbors. Learn about each other, do simple things together.

Remember how to be playful. Break out the cards and board games. Watch children play. They are good teachers.

Sing, play music, hum, whistle. Sound is a powerful healer.

And most of all, love. Yourself, your friends, your family, your pets, anyone, everyone.

I wonder:

Many years ago, before the cataclysmic Missoula flood carved out the undulating Palouse country of Eastern Washington, if a wandering prophet told people that a huge wall of water was coming, would they have moved to higher ground? It wouldn't have made sense to people that fifty-five cubic miles of water would rage over the valley in just 48 hours.

So let's be prepared for the unexpected, the unreasonable. Maybe by attending to our inner stirrings we'll find our own higher ground.

#

Marilyn Trail is on the faculty of Washington State University Cooperative Extension in Spokane County, focusing on building resilience in youth, families and community. She is the chair of the local arrangements for the 1999 Community Development Society's annual conference to be held in Spokane in July, 1999. She received an AB degree from Vassar College, where she studied mathematics and philosophy, preparing her for work in the new field of computer programming and systems analysis. She worked for Shell Oil, the Army Corps of Engineers and the University of Colorado's Joint Institute for Laboratory Astrophysics. After marriage, two children and divorce, she earned a M.A. in Clinical and Social Psychology. She raised her children, Eric and Gretchen Kuhner, on Bainbridge Island, Wash., where she was a counselor in private practice.

Waste Equals Food

Our Future and the Making of Things

BY WILLIAM MCDONOUGH

If Y2K interrupts business-as-usual, and industry grinds to a halt, will we have any choice in how it starts up again? If in fact we will, then I hope we could incorporate the design principles detailed below. The following is edited from a speech given at the Environmental Forum for Business in April 1997, in Spokane, Washington. Although William McDonough was not specifically addressing Y2K, his thoughts are remarkably pertinent for our consideration. —J.L.

I'm going to talk today about design because I'm a designer. And there's an old joke that when all you have is a hammer, everything starts to look like a nail. Well, as a designer, everything looks like a design problem to me, so today I'd like to talk about design and design problems. And I'd to be a little bit assertive and perhaps break some new ground here.

I'd like to look at redesigning design itself. It's interesting that I come now from Charlottesville, Virginia, where I live in a house designed by Thomas Jefferson, because we get to think often about Mr. Jefferson at "the University," as we call it. I think that he saw himself as a designer as well. All you have to do is to look at his tombstone, which he designed, and which has three things noted on it. It says "Thomas Jefferson. Author of the Declaration of American Independence. Author of the Statute of Religious Freedom for the State of Virginia." Which matured into the Bill of Rights. And "Father of the University of Virginia."

Notice he's only recording his legacy, not his activity. No mention of being twice President, Secretary of State, Governor of Virginia, Minister to France. Simply recording legacy rather than activity. And if we see that from a design perspective, we realize that when the Exxon Valdez disaster occurred, the GNP measurements of Prince William Sound went up, because there were so many people there cleaning up. So as long as our measuring system simply measures our activity and not our legacy, the instructions to our design, which I see as the first signal of human intention, aren't necessarily the right signals.

And so I'd like us to consider a series of what I call "Retroactive Design Assignments," because I'm going to posit that all of the people in this room are also designers, because you all have intentions, you all put them into play. And I'd like to give us some retroactive design assignments.

But the two that I want to float before I go into the body of the talk are: "How can you love all the children?"—not just your children, or some of the children—but all of the children when you make a design decision. And as an architect I have to also ask this question, "Why can't I design a building just like a tree?"

If Jefferson were a designer, what would be the design assignment of the Declaration of Independence? Could you author a document that calls for life, liberty and the pursuit of happiness free from remote tyranny? That would be the retroactive design assignment of the Declaration of Independence. In Jefferson's time, remote tyranny would be represented by a person, George III, for example. Someone who didn't understand local conditions and made decisions that were untenable. Remote tyranny.

Well, I would posit that if [someone like] Thomas Jefferson came back today, she would come back calling for Declarations of <u>Inter</u>dependence. And the issue would be the same. How could we have life, liberty and the pursuit of happiness? Can you imagine our current Congress using the word "happiness" in a bill? Life, liberty and the pursuit of happiness free from what I call inter-generational remote tyranny. Because from a design perspective, I think we have a problem in the way we take, the way we make, and the way we use things.

Now I think Jefferson understood this concept of inter-generational remote tyranny. In fact, I know he did, because in 1789 he wrote a letter to James Madison. In it he said, "The earth belongs to the living. No man may by natural right oblige the lands he owns or occupies to debts greater than those that may be paid during his own lifetime. Because if he could, then the world would belong to the dead and not to the living."

The world would belong to the dead.

Oren Lyons, chief of the Onondaga people told me that Ben-

The Iroquois' Great Peacemaker instructed his chiefs that they should make all decisions on behalf of their seventh generation.

jamin Franklin spoke Mohawk. Jefferson studied the Iroquois Confederacy, and the Iroquois Confederacy was brought together by their Great Peacemaker. And their Great Peacemaker instructed his chiefs that they should make all decisions on behalf of their seventh generation, even if it required them to have skin as thick as the bark of a pine.

I think it's clear that Jefferson was writing the Declaration of Independence for his seventh generation, because it's interesting to note that the people sitting in this room *are* Thomas Jefferson's seventh generation. We are it.

And so it's our turn to write declarations of interdependence for our seventh generation.

The founding fathers, in all their wisdom and acuity, would never have given an individual, a company, or a government, the right to slowly poison the planet and kill children. When did we think we had the right to do that? It would never have been put in the Bill of Rights because they would never have imagined that we would even think to do such a thing. Thomas Jefferson lived in a world that was solar powered. Oil had not been discovered yet.

And so we need a retroactive design assignment, and we need to look at some new designs based on ethics, based on ethical principles. This is all about doing good business. Because we need to separate the moral dimension, I think, from our fundamental engine of change, which is commerce itself.

But before I get into the relationship of commerce and design, I'd like you to think about a design assignment for me while I go into this. And I want you to consider whether or not this is an ethical assignment. Am I asking you to do something that's ethical? Could you design an industrial system for this country that produces billions of pounds of highly hazardous toxic material and puts it in your soil, your air and your water every year? Could you design a system of production that measures productivity by how few people are working? Measures prosperity by how much of your natural capital you can cut down, dig up, bury, burn, and otherwise destroy? Measures progress by your number of smokestacks and, if you're especially proud of them, put your name on them? Requires thousands of complex regulations to keep you from killing each other too quickly? And while you're at it, produce a few items so highly toxic that they'll require thousands of generations to maintain constant vigilance while living in terror? Can you do that? Is that an ethical assignment?

If design is a signal of human intention, who designed this? Did we intend for this to happen? I don't think so. I don't think this is the result of design. This is a result of thousands, millions of tiny decisions based on fundamental self interests that have amalgamated into a retroactive design assignment that's obviously questionable from an ethical perspective.

So let's give ourselves a new set of design assignments. Wouldn't it be wonderful if we could design things that didn't produce any hazardous material that is put into our soil, our air, and our water? Wouldn't it be wonderful to measure productivity by how many people are working? Prosperity by how much natural capital and solar income we can accrue and put into closed cycles of investment for future generations? To measure our progress by how many buildings have *no* pipes? Wouldn't it be wonderful if we didn't require regulations at all because we're not trying to kill each other? If we didn't produce anything that results in inter-generational remote tyranny?

Basically we've seen capitalism, socialism and all the dialogue of where we are in between. And we've seen that socialism certainly hasn't been good for the environment. Russia's chief scientist has declared that 16 percent of the Russian land mass is uninhabitable. We see that pure capitalism is not good for the environment because its interest is too isolated.

What has been missing is what the chemist Michael Braungart and I call ecologism. We haven't been factoring the environment into that dialogue. We have three points that have to be accommodated: economy, equity, and ecology. But an ecologistic response would be just as dangerous as a pure capitalist or a pure socialist response. Any "ism" is dangerous. The Germans have an example of this. Look at an ecologistic response from an industrial perspective as a design failure. Watch this slide.

They set up a new recycling system for waste—you've probably heard of it, the take-back law in Germany. If you make something, you have to be able to take it back. And they went to the Tetrapak Company, the people who make juice boxes, those little packages made of plastic, paper and aluminum. And they said, "You must recycle." Ecologism. You must recycle. And so Tetrapak has spent $2 billion building recycling plants to recycle those packages. It's costing them three and a half times as much to recycle one of them as it costs to make one.

And what are we getting out of these recycled packages? We're getting flower pots, park benches, building materials. I don't want plastic and aluminum in my walls. Why are we taking what we would call technical nutrients and burying them in our buildings? The problem is, that package was never designed to be recycled. This is way too aggressive a response, to make people recycle something that was never designed to be recycled.

And so we have to be careful to balance these three issues of ecology, equity and economy without being extreme in any position.

If we're going to need a new design assignment, we better find out how to work within the natural world that we inhabit. I was asked by the city of Hannover, Germany in 1991 to write the design principles for the World's Fair for the year 2000. They're called the Hannover Principles and we can get copies for you if you'd like them. In it we explore the question of the relationship between humanity, nature and technology—the theme of the World's Fair.

So the first question is, "What is Nature?" And if we go back in history, we can see Emerson effectively asking the question in 1836: "If human beings are natural, are therefore all things made by human beings natural?" And his conclusion was that nature is all those things that are immutable, things that are too large for humans to affect, in his words, "the oceans, the mountains, and the leaves."

I think Thoreau understood, and we now understand, that we can indeed affect the oceans. Just ask Jacques Cousteau. We can indeed affect the mountains. Just look around. And we can indeed affect the leaves. Go to the Adirondacks.

And so we realize that perhaps we have been given a kind of dominion over nature. There's been a debate about how unfortunate it was that Genesis talks about God giving humans dominion over the world. And people ask, "Isn't it too bad it wasn't stewardship?" Well, I would have to posit, isn't stewardship implicit within dominion? Because how can you have dominion over something you've killed?

And ultimately the question is perhaps the Native American question, which is not really even stewardship, because that's still anthropocentric. Perhaps the question is, how do we find ourselves in kinship with nature? How do we find ourselves as part of nature? How do we find a rightful, meaningful place within nature?

Well, what is design? If design is the first signal of intention, what is our intention? What designs do we have? Let's look at Emerson again in the 1830s. He went to Europe after his wife died, and he went over on a sailboat and returned in a steamship. Now let's abstract this for fun. He went over on his solar powered recyclable craft operated by craftspersons practicing ancient arts in the open air. And he returned in a steel rust bucket, putting oil on the water, smoke into the sky, operated by people working in the darkness, shoveling fossil fuels into the mouth of a boiler.

These are designs. And guess what? We're still designing steamships. We are in a steamship right now. The sun is shining out there and we're in here, producing nuclear isotopes, carbon dioxide, chewing up rivers. And we're sitting in the dark for all intents and purposes. So from a design perspective we are still in the dark, shoveling fossil fuels into the mouth of a boiler. We need a new design.

Who is going to do this? Us. All of us. We're all designers here. Peter Senge at the Sloan School of Management at MIT has something called a learning laboratory where they study how organizations learn how to learn. And within that he has a leadership lab where they bring in CEOs, Chairs, and so on, and his first question to them is, "Who is the leader on a ship crossing the ocean?" Everybody comes back with captain, navigator, helmsman, chef. And he says, "No. The leader on a ship is the designer of the ship." Because you could be the best captain in the world, but if the ship isn't designed to be seaworthy, and you get caught in a storm, you're going down. His point is that leaders must become designers. Designers must become leaders.

Now what I'm talking about here—I'm going to be a little aggressive—I am *not* talking about eco-efficiency. The thing that separates me, I think, from all of my colleagues is that I'm actually not that interested in eco-efficiency. I think eco-efficiency's wonderful and it's very important, but ultimately I'm focusing on the design assignment. And so I'll be a bit strident about this.

If we look at the development of species, we realize that nature is not efficient. Everybody talks about how we should model ourselves on nature because it's so efficient. I even get written up as a person who models his designs on the efficiency of natural systems. But nature's not efficient. Nature's effective.

I took a walk this morning with Dave Crockett onto your fairgrounds over here and we walked by a cherry tree in full bloom. And I thought about it and I said, "I'm going to talk about this tree this morning." I don't look at that tree and wag my finger and say, "Boy, are you inefficient. Look at all those cherry blossoms." You know, "How many does it take?" The thing that's nice about nature is that it's safe. We don't care if there's a lot more blossoms than necessary. Nature is abundant. Nature celebrates itself. Nature is beautiful because it's effective, not efficient. But everything it makes is safe and it returns to the soil. It returns to natural cycles, so we're not afraid of it. Humans are trying so hard to be efficient because the stuff we make is typically so dangerous, you *have* to be efficient about making it.

Look at all the men in this room. A hundred million sperm in each one of you, just in case a couple of them get lucky. You're not very efficient. So I'd rather celebrate the world as a world of abundance, rather than a world full of limits. When I gave the closing address to EPA, for their 33/50 program on voluntary toxic reductions, I was standing there with some of our clients. And they were getting awards for 90 percent reduction of toxins over five years, for example. And I said, "Well, you know, the only problem with this from a design perspective is that we've got Zeno's Paradox here."

Zeno's Paradox is about the fact that an arrow on its way to a target can always been seen as being halfway there. You can always say, "Stop. Freeze frame." The arrow can be halfway to its target at any given moment. Therefore, it never gets there. That's the paradox. Because it can always be seen as halfway at a certain point in time.

In a way, eco-efficiency has a similar built-in paradox. Because now that you've got your reduction by 90 percent, guess what? You've got a new 100 percent. You're never going to reach your target.

At the same time, we're starting to see EPA changing its regulations to start to focus on safe levels for children instead of adults because children are not small adults. They have different surface to volume ratios. They breathe through their mouths and not their noses. Things get directly to their lungs without being filtered, and so on. And all of a sudden we realize, also, that microscopic particles of man-made materials are now causing questionable effects in our endocrine systems; that parts per billion, even parts per trillion—seemingly infinitesimal amounts—of these things can cause serious problems. And so the question has to be, "Why are we making these things in the first place? Can't we really *redesign*?"

I like to use Dave Crockett's driving analogy to illuminate this point. When I leave Charlottesville, I can go north to Washington or I can go south to Lynchburg. If I find myself going 100 miles an hour toward Washington, but I'm supposed to be going to Lynchburg, it's no help to me to slow down to 20 miles per hour. Because I'll still be going in the wrong direction. I have to turn around.

What I'd like to do is talk about that turning around. I'd also like to look at the issues of energy and mass. Remember Einstein's equation had two sides: $E = mc^2$. I think we're going to solve the energy problem because we do have current solar income. I don't think we're going to solve the mass problem: the problem of the loss of genetic information and the problem of persistent toxification.

There are 500 manmade chemicals that nature never saw before that are in our fatty tissue and in the fatty tissue of animals all over the planet including Antarctica. This is something we will not be able to change, certainly not within thousands of lifetimes. It's persistent. It's pernicious. It's bioaccumulative. And we are doing a mass experiment that we have no idea how to stop.

If we're going to need design principles, what would be the retroactive design principle of the first industrial revolution? The only one I've been able to figure out is that, "If brute force doesn't work, you're not using enough of it." That seems about it. In architecture we design the same building in Reykjavik and Rangoon. We heat one; we cool the other. If you're not hot enough, add energy. If you're not cold enough, add energy. One size fits all. If brute force doesn't work, you're not using enough of it.

We need some richer design principles. I use three in my work. And they are *waste equals food*, *use current solar income*, and *respect diversity*.

Waste equals food. I coined this term and also use the term *cradle to cradle* to describe the way we design with life cycle in mind. And the life cycle is not what Michael Braungart and I have characterized as "downcycling." It's true recycling. Right now we're making park benches out of our plastics. This is good news for the homeless. It's bad news for the rest of us. We figured out we're making about 83 park benches per capita right now. This is downcycling. This is not recycling. This is taking valuable technical materials and sending them to the landfill as they stop off as a park bench on their way there.

We need to design for true recycling, so that waste equals food.

Use current solar income. Nature doesn't mine the past; it doesn't borrow from the future. It uses current income. So should we. You'll see that all our buildings are daylit.

Respect diversity. Look at the people in this room. No two people are the same. No two places in the world are the same. No two cultural flows, spiritual flows, materials flows, energy flows are the same anywhere. Why are we designing one size fits all? Why can't we design working with local conditions, working with local culture, and celebrate natural energy and material flows?

Well, if waste equals food, then there's no such thing as waste. If there's no such thing as waste, and everything is food, then food are nutrients and therefore they are nutrients of metabolisms. And so what are the metabolisms with which we work? I have mentioned I work with a chemist named Michael Braungart. We've started a company called McDonough Braungart Design Chemistry, and we design processes and systems for industries. We're working with a whole raft of industries right now, with major corporations. This is not marginal. This is big business.

We say there are two fundamental metabolisms. There's the organic one, the one we physically inhabit and reside in, the world of nature. The other we call the technical metabolism. It's the metabolism of human industry. We should design things to go into either the organic cycle or to the technical cycle, and we should design nothing else. Everything else we would call an unmarketable because it can't return to these cycles.

Watch what happens when you start to design like this. I'll go through some projects to explain what happens. There are two characteristics you need to know. One is that if you end up with what we call a Product of Consumption the thing gets truly consumed. That means it goes to an organic cycle.

Let's look at this notion of "consumers" for a moment. I came to the United States from the Far East, and I spent my childhood summers in the Puget Sound. My father's from Washington. But I used to come here from Hong Kong, and I was always amazed that in America we had stopped being people with lives at some point and we had become consumers with lifestyles. When did that happen?

Even on television they talk about "consumers" this and "consumers" that. How do you consume a TV set? If I had a television set hidden in this podium and I said, "I have this amazing object, it provides an incredible service. But before I tell you what it does, let me tell you what it is. You tell me if you want this in your house. It's 4,360 chemicals. It has large amounts of toxic heavy metals. It has an explosive glass tube. And we think you ought to put it eye level with your children and encourage them to play with it. Do you want this in your house? Why are we selling people hazardous waste?

Future generations will look back and say, "What did you do with all those valuable technical nutrients? The chromium, the antimony, the mercury, the lead? Why were you taking all these materials and then dispersing them into little holes all over the planet so that we'll never be able to get them back, while you persistently toxify the earth's surface? What were you thinking? What was your design intention?"

And so we advise people to design things to go back to soil safely with no mutagens, no carcinogens, no heavy metals, no persistent toxins, no bioaccumulative substances, no endocrine disrupters.

Otherwise, design things to be what we call Products of Service. Something that is designed to provide you with a service, like a television set. But when you've finished with it, you've effectively leased it from the manufacturer, and it goes back to them because it is now designed to become a TV again, forever. And so our clients include companies that make televisions, computers, cars, shoes, carpets, fabrics. And we're designing all of these products so that they will go back to the industries from whence they came so that waste equals food. Whose food is this waste? It's the food of the electronics industry, in the case of a TV set. It's the food of an automobile industry in the case of a car. Amazing things start to happen to the design once you take on this protocol.

We also need to enrich our criteria. Typically the design criteria that we've all used are cost, performance, and aesthetics. Can I afford it? Does it work? Do I like it? Or in architecture school we reverse that. We do aesthetics, performance, and cost. But it doesn't matter. Still the same three. We need to enrich that by adding three new ones. Is it ecologically intelligent? Is it just? And is it fun?

And now I'd like to show you some projects quickly. And we'll discuss them in terms of their ecological intelligence, their justness and their fun.

(Shows slides.)

This is a fabric. We were asked by DesignTex, part of the Steelcase Corporation, the largest manufacturer of office furniture in America, to design a new fabric for furniture along with Richard Meier, Aldo Rossi from Italy, Robert Venturi, Denise Scott Brown— some very well-known architects, known for their design. We were honored to be in that company, but we said, "You know, we're going to have to design not only what it looks like but also what it *is*." And their director said, "Yes, we figured you'd say something like that and we are delighted at the prospect. So we've already figured it out for you to help move this along. And we're going to propose to mix cotton, which is natural, with PET from Coke bottles, which is recycled. And that way we have natural and recycled. We've got all the buzzwords. It's cheap. It's durable. It works fine. What do you think?"

Well, what do you think? Is that a good product? Is that something we should make? Based on our criteria, is that an organic nutrient? Does that go back to soil safely? Not with the PET. Is it going to go back to technical cycles? Not with the cotton. Isn't that interesting? A product that should not be made. How many times have you heard that? Can you imagine people sitting around the room going, "Oh, well, there's another one we shouldn't make"? Wouldn't it be great if this kind of discussion was going on with genetic engineering? You know, some wizard sitting there saying, "Gee you know we could cross the animal kingdom with the plant kingdom. God never tried it. But maybe we could." Wouldn't it be nice if somebody is sitting in the room said, "Well, somehow I don't think we should try that one. Because we don't know what that's going to mean."

And they call this science? You do the experiment, release it into the world, then you watch what happens and talk about it. Remember PCBs and CFCs? Amazing! This is actually primitive science, a non-ecologically intelligent product design.

Let's look at it from a deeper perspective. Cotton requires over 20 percent of the world's pesticide use. It causes hydrological disasters. Goodbye Aral Sea. And it has never been associated with social fairness. PET is a petrochemical full of anti-oxidants, UV stabilizers, plasticizers, antimony residues from catalytic reactions. It was not designed to be next to human skin.

Why would I want to put these two things together?

So, for DesignTex, we decided to do an organic nutrient, a fabric we did in Switzerland at the most advanced mill there. They're trying to be an eco-mill, doing their eco-efficiency reductions, trying to get their cadmium levels down to thresholds and so on and so forth. I talked to the president and I said, "You know, wouldn't it be great if waste equals food?"

The previous week the trimmings of his bolts of cloth had been declared by the Swiss government to be hazardous waste. They couldn't be buried or burned in Switzerland. He had to export them to Spain. Now, we've hit the wall of the first industrial revolution when the trimmings of your product are declared hazardous waste, but you can sell what's in the middle. You don't need to be Einstein to work out what it is you're selling. The most eco-efficient thing he could have done is sell the product untrimmed. Because the customers are going to cut it up anyway. So he realized what his problem was. I said, "Wouldn't it be great if the trimming of your bolts of cloth became compost for the local garden club? So let's design that." And he did a magnificent job. Over the course of a year we developed a fabric based on the idea that people have to sit and be warm in winter, cool in summer. We designed a fabric using wool, which is an absorber—it absorbs 30 percent of its volume in water—and ramie, which is a nettle family plant from the Philippines, organically grown. And the wool is from happy sheep in New Zealand.

We designed it based on interviewing people in wheelchairs, because we considered that worst-case sitting, and it turns out their biggest problem is moisture buildup. So we designed a fabric that absorbs moisture and then wicks it away. It's a structural fiber stronger than steel in tension when it's wet. It absorbs the water and then wicks it away. After we had done that, we had the process. But now we had to make it beautiful, and make the colors and so on. And we said, you know the filters of the future, our design filters, we're not going to put them on the ends of pipes and chimneys. We're going to put filters in our heads. More intelligence. Less stuff. And the filter is this: no mutagens, no carcinogens, no heavy metals, no persistent toxins, no bioaccumulatives, no endocrine disrupters.

We went to 60 chemical companies in Europe and said, "Who wants to put their products through our filter?" Within three days, they'd shut us down. It was amazing how quickly they talked to each other. Everybody was going around, "Are you going to do it?" "No, no." "Are you going to do it?" "No, no, no." Three days. "Sorry." Nobody was going to do it. So we went to Ciba Geigy in Basel, and we explained our idea. Michael Braungart and his team looked at 8,000 chemicals in the textile industry and, with that filter, had to eliminate 7,962. We were left with 38 chemicals out of 8,000. We did the entire fabric line with only those 38 chemicals. It's won gold medals. It's in the marketplace. It's a big success. It exists, therefore it is possible.

Now the ironic part was that we had every color we wanted except black. Remember Henry Ford's first industrial revolution, "You can have any color you want as long as it's black"? Now you can have any color you want as long as it's NOT black. (We've since figured out black.)

But the part that's really exciting to me from a design perspective is that after the fabric was in production, the factory's director called me and said, "Listen. You have to know what happened when we ran your protocol." The Swiss inspectors had come to test the water as they are required to do legally every day. And they thought their equipment had broken. They checked the water coming into the plant and, sure enough, the equipment was fine. It was Swiss drinking water. It turned out that the fabrics were filtering the water. The water coming out of the factory was as clean as the water going in.

Now the implications of this are astonishing when your effluent is as clean as your influent, which is Swiss drinking water. You can then use your effluent for process. And guess what happens then? You cap the pipe. That's what the mill is going to do now. There will be no effluent from this factory. There will be nothing to regulate. Nothing to measure. Why? Because they're not trying to kill anybody.

This fabric is what we consider the flag of what Michael and our friend and collaborator, Paul Hawken, call the Next Industrial Revolution.

We're now applying these concepts to carpets with Interface Inc. The idea is that they'll take carpets back forever. We're also working with the Herman Miller company. We did a new factory for them in Zeeland, Michigan. It's right next to a site with sculpted lawns and a few Canada geese and a couple of pine trees and then a big metal building. There's a big pond with a pump fountain. We looked at that and said, "Do an inventory of biodiversity." Two species of flora: pine and fescue. One species of fauna: Canada geese, unloved. The grass was being hacked back as it tried to go to seed. It was really quite an ironic message when you think about it. We pump grass full of fertilizers and then hack it back every time it tries to grow. Then we poison it to make sure that nothing else can enjoy its presence.

On our site, the water travels through swales all over the site, so it produces absolutely no storm water problems. It's called the "roly poly site." We now have great blue herons nesting, egrets and songbirds. We decided to measure our success by how many songbirds return to the site. It's made with local materials as much as possible. It's a factory for recycling furniture, forever.

We engaged everyone in the factory in the design of the building from day one. It was designed and built within 18 months, one week off schedule—early. And it was exactly on budget to the penny. It was ten percent more than a normal building: $48 a square foot instead of a metal Butler building, which is $44 a square foot in Michigan. We used all local materials, which has multiplier effects in the local economy. But the part that's really interesting is that we created an urbane situation in a sub-urbane place. The bottom of the plan is where the offices are and the factory is in the back. And where they meet is a street, so that people spend their day bumping into each other along a street. If anyone wants to get a cup of coffee or have meetings or whatever, they meet on a street. We actually brought daylight into the building with glare.

We celebrate glare. Engineers are always worried about this stuff. They say, "No. We have to neutralize everything." So you end up with buildings with no windows. And we said, "No. Let the employees control the shade." So the people on the factory lines have clickers and they can aim at a window if sun's in their eyes. They can click, aim at it, and the shade comes down for half an hour. Then it goes back up. They control it themselves. They never have to turn the lights on during the full daylight hours. We had Battelle National Labs analyze this company for productivity for a year before they moved. And they've been in now for over a year. The result is what we expected and we're very excited about it. But listen to this. Many people told us at the beginning that they didn't expect productivity improvement because this company was so spunky. They figured it was already 95 percent productive. Well, they've monitored it for a year and it looks like they've increased productivity by over one percent. [Lately I have been told overall productivity is up over 20% in the company. —W.M.]

One percent may not seem like much, but if you make $250 million worth of furniture every year, and you pick up a one percent productivity increase—we know it's from the building, and we know it's the daylight because it came from the first two shifts, it didn't come from the night shift—that increase is worth $2.5 million a year with the same employee cost. Now, amortize the extra profit with the financing, and you could finance the building improvements in no time. Someone at Herman Miller told me that William McDonough & Partners gave them the building as a present.

So when people say to us, "How do you talk your clients into spending ten percent more?" we're not talking about changing a few light bulbs. The cost of the building is insignificant next to the value of people. For example, people can see what they're doing. The roof has these monitors so there's daylight everywhere. They can see what their work looks like. They can look under their bench when they drop something, and they feel like they spent their day outdoors.

This slide is a competition we won for a corporate campus in San Bruno, California. We're a small firm: they called us "the kids." We competed against the two largest companies in America, HOK and Gensler, and we won. It was a fun competition because the assignment from the chairman of the company wasn't a specific pro-

We decided we would design the building from the air, so that a bird would look down and say, "This is nice."

gram, it was to design a concept for a building. Don't design a building. We didn't have to worry about where the bathrooms were. We had to design a *concept for a building*. This is the last green site in San Bruno, California. We decided we would design the building from the air, so that a bird would look down and say, "This is nice."

The roof is grass. The roof is the oak savanna of the original landscape. And we saved all the live oaks that are on the site, every one, and then designed the building around them with this giant meadow. And we won the competition and made the design real, broke it into two phases. It'll open this fall [1997]. It has an undulating grass roof and daylighting everywhere.

Now the metaphor here is that from the air, the roof is the earth. So as far as birds are concerned, nothing happened. There's no storm water problems as a result of this building, because it still absorbs and makes oxygen. The roof is absorbing water and making oxygen. But from the inside, it's a giant undulating curve because we've been able to use raised floors for air and for computer access. And nobody wants to pay for that — it costs more for raised floors.

But our idea was to use the raised floor to move nighttime air through the floor all night to cool down the slabs of the building. So we actually use the nighttime coolness of San Francisco to cool the building. We get free cooling. We were able to cut the mechanical equipment by over half and the energy bills by well over half. And that paid for the raised floor and left the ceiling clean. People feel like they've spent their day outdoors. The entire building is daylit, so we're not adding heat and then having to air condition it out, which is what typically happens in office buildings today.

This slide is the new Environmental Studies Center for Oberlin College in Ohio, and the question here is the one I posed earlier: "Why can't a building be like a tree?" Let me give you the retroactive design assignment of a tree. Could you design something for me that purifies water, provides habitat for hundreds of species, builds soil, accrues solar income as fuel, provides food and micro-climate, makes oxygen, fixes nitrogen and sequesters carbon? Can you do that for me? How many buildings do you know that produce oxygen? Wouldn't it be amazing if we could design a building like a tree? Compared to a tree, our buildings are incredibly crude.

So that's what we're doing at Oberlin; we gave ourselves a design challenge with David Orr, the head of Environmental Studies there, to design a building that's a net energy exporter. The idea is, the building would produce more energy than it needs to operate and it becomes fecund and it gives something back. Because if sustainability is simply maintenance, if it's just going to be that edge between destruction and restoration, then all we're giving our children as a legacy is maintenance. Ultimately, that's an impoverished agenda because it's like eco-efficiency.

If I look at eco-efficiency as a design assignment, what would it be? I'd have to say, "I wake up in the morning feeling really bad. I spend my day trying to feel better by being less bad and my goal is zero." Is this fun? I'd rather look at it and say, "What does 100 percent sustainable look like?" I'd rather wake up in the morning and say, "I'm only 21 percent sustainable today. Tomorrow I'd like to be 22." Because that means I'd have to imagine what 100 percent looks like. It means I have to re-imagine the world. That we don't accept it as it is and just try and be less bad about it. We actually posit what 100 percent good would look like and get onto that track.

This slide shows an experimental project to articulate the concept of a building like a tree. On the north side there are offices. That's a grass roof that absorbs the water of the building. The big wing of a roof is south facing; it has solar collectors; it has photovoltaics which produce as much energy as is needed to run the building and then some. On the south side, in the lobby at the bottom of the drawing, is a living machine designed by John Todd, a marine biologist. It's a botanical garden that purifies all the water waste of the building to drinking water standards. So the building actually purifies its own water and accrues solar energy.

It is fully daylit, and it has natural ventilation systems. We're working with Amory Lovins and his teams to develop energy systems that I think will astonish you. If you want to get into detail, I'd be happy to talk to you about them.

This is a project we're doing in Indiana, outside Gary and Chesterton, Indiana. It's a new community on a square mile of land, an extension of a small town. But the reason I want to show it to you is that the real estate developer who did golf course developments asked one of the largest real estate advisories in the world to tell him what the future looked like way out ahead of the curve. We were brought in to look at it. We spent a day with them. And a year later they called up and said, "Okay, let's do it."

This slide shows what we got when we arrived there. This is four-lane highways leading to arterials leading to subdivisions with cul-de-sacs—the original plan. We transformed it into a pedestrian-oriented community. These are all neighborhoods with gardens, with parks. We're redesigning retail commerce itself. We're using the concept of distribution inherent in a Wal-Mart to solve the problem created by a Wal-Mart, basically letting them do custom distribution to Mom and Pop stores within each neighborhood. So everybody will be able to walk to one of those little red corner stores and get whatever they need.

The houses will have south-facing roofs and the utility will rent their space and the entire town will be photovoltaic. It will be its own utility. The solar collectors will be provided as Products of Service by the utility. In other words, people aren't going to have to be asked to buy ugly blue rectangles made of heavy metal combinations. They'll be asked to rent their south-facing surfaces for energy and then some. We have a global positioning transit system. The transit vehicles will know where you are and will be able to pick you up and take you anywhere you want to go. We've even got horse-drawn carriages that'll move though here, because $8 a day worth of oats is a lot cheaper than running off to Saudi Arabia. There are only 600 breeding pair of Percherons left, which is unfortunate, so we'll bring some of them back.

There's a transit loop that moves through it and makes it very convenient. And the point here is that if you look at a young family in America trying to get a house, the cheapest thing they can afford right now is a double-wide on the nearest acre at the fringe. That's what cancer looks like under a microscope if you look at that from the air. What we realized is, it's not just our subdivisions, it's actually this creeping requirement of our people to go to affordable housing, because that's all we have to offer.

We need to spend more time with our kids. Remember that question: "How do you love all the children?" By design. We're forcing people into remote circumstance. All of a sudden, if there are two parents and kids, you've got to have two cars because you can't leave people isolated. The average car in America costs $7,000 a year. So that's $14,000 a year going into cars for that family. Both of those parents have to work, and one of them is working for the cars, because after taxes $14,000 is a living wage.

What we're saying is, wouldn't it be wonderful if that family didn't need two cars because of a transit system, and they could have just one car? What would the implication be? Well, free up $7,000 a year and see what it's worth. It's worth $70,000 worth of mortgage. So instead of somebody being stuck with a $50,000 double wide on the fringe costing incredible services from the county and causing sprawl, they could be living in a $120,000 house financed by their not having to have that car, or the other person doesn't have to work. They could stay with the children if they wanted to. All of a sudden we realize that our families can go back to being families and not to being chauffeurs or consumers of tires, gasoline, automobiles, etcetera.

We studied the prairie of Indiana and it turns out — these are the roots of prairie grasses; they're up to 16 feet deep — it turns out that the prairie was a giant sponge. There was no such thing as runoff. The upper Mississippi reaches were all fed by groundwater. So the entire community is being designed to absorb water everywhere. There are no gutters. There are no concrete curbs. The roads are all brick. They're 22 feet wide instead of 44 feet wide. And all the surfaces are being designed to absorb water. (In our office we see "asphalt" as two words assigning blame.)

So I guess what I'm saying here is that if we ask, "Why can't a building be like a tree?" we find ourselves doing amazing things and rediscovering the creative joys of designing. I'll give you one quick example. On the Oberlin building, when we first did the runs, it turned out that it was only 43 percent solar-powered. Amory and I asked, "Where's all the energy being used?" A lot of it was in the pumps driving the system, because the south side of the building was used to heat the north side. Two ground-connected heat pumps were linked, so they actually used the heat built up on the south to heat the north, etc. We looked at the pumps and said, "You know, what if we change the way we design?"

Most engineers sit and do the piping diagram. They try to save material and so they'll say, this is a half-inch pipe, this is this and that, and they add it all up. They find out what the friction loss is and then put in a five horsepower pump to run the water through the system. We said, "What if we reverse the design? What if we designed it from the pump out?" In other words, what if we design for zero friction? What if all the pipes got bigger because the real job is the sweating of the joints, etc. It's not the cost of the pipe; whether it's this big or that big is almost irrelevant in terms of overall cost.

So we designed it without friction. The pump sizes dropped by 95 percent. Because what you realize is that we're going to pay for those pumps in energy consumption over and over and over again. In fact, we're going to spend as much on energy as the pump cost — in one year. What if we could actually design the system so that it was frictionless? In other words, there's a nice metaphor here. Let's remove stress. Let's get rid of friction. Let's let our systems go limp. Let's make them fun and friendly. All of a sudden you realize that the building could easily power itself—because we had taken the stress out of the system.

It never would have occurred to us to do this until we realized we only had this finite energy budget. That forced us to rethink the way we design systems.

So the essential questions are, "Why can't a building be like a tree?" In other words, why are we here in this steamship?

And "How can we love our children, all of the children?" When you ask yourself that question, interesting things happen to design.

I'll close with a story from Curitiba, Brazil. Jaime Lerner, the former mayor and now the governor of the state of Parana, was recently at the university because he won the Thomas Jefferson medal in architecture, the highest prize in architecture in the world, as far as we're concerned anyway.

When Curitiba had a visit from the former mayor of Jerusalem, he said to the mayor, Rafael Greco, at the time, "Where's your library?" They realized Curitiba didn't have a library. Here's a city trying to keep up with expanding growth. They've gone from 600,000 to almost two million since 1970. And they didn't have a library. So the consensus was, "Oh, we've got to do a library." Instead of doing what San Francisco did, a $150 million mausoleum for books at the Civic Center, the question was, "How do you build a library and love all the children?" They realized that a central library wasn't going to be any good to most of the children, because they wouldn't be able to get there, they wouldn't have time, they wouldn't have money, even though the transit system there is spectacular.

So the question became, "How do you build a library and love all the children?" What they ended up doing was building tiny libraries, the size of little houses, with a lighthouse in front called a "beacon of knowledge." And volunteers sit in this glass room about ten meters up and read books—a fireman, teacher, parent, or forester. They make sure all the kids are safe because these are built within 12 minutes' walking distance of every child in the city. When kids get to this library, this friendly little building, they find all the reference books they need for school. If they can't afford to buy the books that they want to take home for school, they can pick up garbage on their way there and trade it for books.

Every little kid, even the barefoot one coming from the hinterlands that arrives in the city, is loved by the city. Jaime's point is that if we don't love the children, how will they love the city? Every kid in Curitiba is getting access to the World Wide Web. How are we doing here in comparison? That's supposed to be a Third World country.

How do we love all our children? How do we love our seventh generation? How do we design things in such a way that when they look back at us from seven generations hence, they realize that what we were doing was signaling a new intention based on new information that we now have about the acts of human artifice. They will realize that we began at this point in history to start to imagine what it might be like to find a meaningful, rightful, and responsible place within nature—to be in kin with nature—and that we accepted the challenge. #

William McDonough is dean of the School of Architecture at the University of Virginia and a practicing architect for William McDonough & Partners. Besides being a founding member of the American Institute of Architects' Committee on the Environment, he served as lead designer for the Greening of White House initiative. His design work ranges from products to buildings to cities to entire regions. He is the only individual to have won the nation's highest environmental award, the Presidential Award for Sustainable Development. You can reach him at McDonough & Partners in Charlottesville, Virginia, (804) 979-1111.

Ask!

A Psychological & Spiritual Survival Kit for the Year 2000

By Kent Hoffman

If January 1 of the year 2000 ushers in the upheaval and chaos that experts believe is possible, there will be consequences for each of us on every level. In my work I have encountered many people—"just normal crazy folks" like you and me—who have, because of some unexpected difficulty, been plunged into significant psychological crisis. Acute depression, profound anxiety, sleepless nights, obsessive thought, feelings of paranoia, doubt and cynicism about the future—all lie just below the surface for many of us. From my particular vantage point, it is certain that if we are confronted with the level of crisis that Y2K could bring, there will quite literally be millions of people suddenly struggling with severe psychological difficulty.

I believe that the best psychological "survival kit" for such a time is found within a spiritual perspective. The word psychology comes from the Greek word "psyche," which means soul. The word religion comes from the Latin word "ligare," which means connection, and "re," which means "to do again." At the heart of spiritual experience is a core need to be connected. In times of crisis, we must find a setting that allows authentic connection for the vulnerable self within each of us.

DARK NIGHT OF THE SOUL

It was a string of sleepless nights, this one the worst. No breeze to soften the eighty-five degree Southern California heat, sweat covering my entire body. I found myself at two a.m. staring yet again at a ceiling that had become all too familiar over the past six weeks. Night after night, I crawled into bed by ten or eleven, dozed off for twenty or thirty minutes and then awakened to a darkness and dread that had begun to swallow the whole of my life. Worse than any nightmare I could remember, these long days and hopeless nights carried with them a sense of despair that seemed unending.

On this particular night I broke through some protective veneer, a layer of illusion that would have me believe that my life had meaning, that goodness existed, that there was a reason to continue living. Tumbling into empty space, I thought I finally realized a truth too terrible to sustain.

"Things won't get better tomorrow, because things can't get better tomorrow. There is nothing but emptiness everywhere I look, no one to help, nothing to hold onto once any of us stumble into this awful knowing." Looking out the window at an old Volkswagen bus chugging past the apartment building, I muttered, "If only I hadn't taken those goddamn tablets."

When one thinks of the drugs of the early 1970s, Excedrin isn't usually one that springs to mind. All I took was two small white tablets for a headache in the spring of 1972, and I was plunged into a terrible descent. I fit into that small percentage of people who are allergic to the combination of chemicals in this common pain medication. I also fit into a much larger percentage of our population that carries, just below the surface, an unnamed dread that is waiting to be triggered by an unexpected event. From my earliest memories I had guessed that something was profoundly amiss in the world. Now, quite suddenly, I was sure of it.

Things would only get worse. Soon I began a three-month internship in the psychiatric unit at California Women's Prison. There I found dozens of women who were clearly dealing with a similar experience of life. Morning after morning I dragged myself out of bed and ventured into the prison in an attempt to provide hope and meaning to those who seemed to have none. This was, of course, a joke, the blind stumbling over the blind.

As I inquired into the lives of the various women, I found in every instance a history of neglect, abuse and eventual resignation. Darkness was abundant, with no relief in sight.

The weeks turned into months, and my head seemed to fill with cotton guaze. Things began to feel muffled, as if an increasing distance was being placed between the world and myself. As this buffer increased, I experienced more and more isolation from everything and everyone. Finally, having tried crisis counseling with several of the best psychotherapists available, having changed my diet, having exercised and sought out long talks with very concerned friends— none of which helped—I concluded that life on this planet was simply unbearable. Everything was a wasteland, experience without meaning.

And so, on a warm afternoon in early August, I began to make plans to kill myself.

Several days later I walked past the church that my parents had attended when I was a baby. I stepped in and, finding no one present, settled into one of the pews. In the darkness of the sanctuary, the weight of the past months descended upon me. I laughed cynically at the lighted cross above the altar—the naiveté of those who dared believe in something as obviously absent as a caring God! Then, quite suddenly, a visceral rush of dark emotion overcame me with a level of intensity that had been missing for fourteen weeks. I paused, waiting for some indication of what this impulse might be and was surprised to realize it was anger.

"Anger? At whom? At what? There is no one to be angry at," I thought. Then, I shouted at the altar and the barren symbol: "I know you don't exist! I know there is no one here who will listen to me! But damn it, there should be! I'm planning to kill myself because this life is so horrible! Not just for me, but for many of us! That's not how it should be!"

It was at this exact moment in my impassioned soliloquy that I felt another upwelling of rage. Within me was an undeniable truth. "Damn it! Goddamn it! I have worth. I'm sure of it! And I know those women I've been working with—Karen, Darlene, Martha, Leslie—also have the same worth. Sure they've done terrible things. But terrible things have been done to them since they were tiny babies." Their stories flashed through my mind, horrifying details of sexual abuse, physical beatings, imprisonment in basements for days at a time.

"Something is wrong here and it isn't us! We are not bad. We have worth! You have got to do something to help us! I'll be damned if I am going to just give up and check out. I've done everything I know how to do, and it doesn't work. I've tried! Now it's your turn!"

This was certainly not your typical act of pious surrender. But transparent within my rage was an affirmation of two important truths: a recognition of humanity's inherent worth and a realization that I could no longer go on alone. I was profoundly limited and needed to ask—really ask—for help from some power beyond myself.

In the quiet after my outburst I still didn't believe anyone was listening. But if nothing else had been accomplished, I had most definitely gotten my own attention. In the time it took to spill out less than a few hundred words, I had allowed myself an awareness—a gut certainty–that was entirely new. I had claimed something that, until then, had only been a vague hunch, a hidden hope. I accepted my own intrinsic value as a human being. I claimed my birthright, my need for comfort when in need. I also knew, beyond any shadow of a doubt, the worth and birthright of every being on this planet, without exception. And I recognized that each of us needed help from a resource that was most definitely beyond my comprehension.

There is an old proverb that says, "Thirst is all the proof we need to know that water exists." It is actually an empirical formula, a statement of balance within the universe. Left implies right; night suggests day; up has built within it the hint that down exists. Just as it is impossible to swing on only one end of a teeter-totter, need is only half of an equation. In those few moments I perceived—without question—the truth of my need. From that time forward, I honored the vulnerability of every human being.

Within an hour of my cry of distress, my head cleared. For the first time in months, the cobwebs and cotton that had been stuffed into my brain were gently pulled away, and a sense of clarity and dawning hope took their place.

A couple of days later I randomly picked up a book at the library and stumbled across the story of a woman whose journey into depression exactly paralleled my own. She spoke of a "deep dread" and a "yawning boredom" that slowly consumed her, of a desire to die that absorbed her every waking hour. She also spoke of a sudden realization that God was using this "dark night" in the same way that a cellar had to be excavated before a cathedral could be built. The chance occurrence of finding this story, one that was almost a verbatim description of my own, gave me a palpable sense of connection. I began to wonder if I were in the company of a divine presence, one that was available, supportive and responsive.

The coincidences continued. The next week I pulled from my own bookshelf a tiny book written by the Cistercian Monk Thomas Merton—*Contemplative Prayer*—given to me by a friend. When I first received it the year before, I could relate to nothing in it. Now every page spoke to me, each sentence filled with meaning. I savored every opportunity to read it. Merton spoke of dread as "an expression of our insecurity in this earthly life." We should allow ourselves to "be brought naked and defenseless into the center of the dread where we stand alone before God in our nothingness, without explanation, without theories . . . ." In so doing we can find the emergence of "grace and mercy," the mysterious opening into a level of love that we would never allow on our own.

Thus Merton, the hermit who lived his life in the hills of Kentucky, distancing himself from the world in order to more deeply listen to and understand the human condition, comforted me in my anguish. He implored readers to recognize, and even be grateful for, the necessity within whatever crisis they found themselves, realizing that their current difficulty could become the means of discovering the only options that would be of genuine benefit.

Dread had brought me to my knees. I had no choice but to surrender, even though—without knowing it—I had fought this vulnerability throughout my whole life. And here was Merton, exposing my need to remain in control at all costs. It wasn't until I had stumbled into church on the very day that I had given up any hope that I realized how I was trying to solve everything on my own terms. "You can offer to help, but I know you won't really come through," is the way I framed my prayers. This was the cynicism-at-the-core that I learned during childhood in a family where my mother suffered through two divorces before I was thirteen, and both of my fathers disappeared without ever speaking a word of farewell. Even though I sought outside resources, I secretly clung to the need to stay in charge of my own life.

"Now I get it," I said to myself. "My need, while being what I am most afraid to admit, is actually my ally." This dark night isn't like the bully who lived next door to me when I was a kid and beat me sadistically to watch me cry. The universe has actually been conspiring on my behalf, trying to find a way to help me relinquish old patterns of cynicism and despair.

A great, sacred mystery had used my lifelong despondency as a means to offer me a way out of it. Finally able to admit my thirst, I opened myself to the second half of the equation. A loving response. My thirst led me to the proof that water exists.

Now, almost thirty years later, it seems that our entire planet faces the distinct possibility of a similar journey. On one hand, I hope not. But in other ways I wonder about it. Surrounded as we are by a myriad of labor-saving devices, each spinning the illusion that we are capable of living this life happily on our own, we have become blinded to the precarious ways in which we have given over our lives to technology. Our sources of power, our food, our means of transportation, our capacity for communication—on and on—each is dependent upon technological resources beyond our control. At the same time our capacity to build community and relationships that can mutually sustain us has atrophied. Ironically, in our desire to deny our dependence, we have become a people who are exceptionally vulnerable—more so than at any time in human history. When the technologies in which we have placed our faith finally crumble, we will be facing the dilemma of what to do with our inherent vulnerability.

We can't choose to *not* be vulnerable. From the time of birth, as we lay waiting for the tender response of our parents, each of us has faced the unavoidable fact of our genuine need. As a psychotherapist, over and over again I have watched that vulnerability lead in one of two directions. Either we feel a need for increased self-protection and move toward further self-sufficiency (in couples and in families, a decision toward rigid self-protection leads to the destruction of the relationship), or we openly admit our need and seek to be in relationship with those who will honor and encourage us. The latter option usually requires some guidance. The open sharing of needs with others involves risk, but so does self-protection. In my experience, sharing yourself leads in the direction of creative options, while self-protection is a dead-end. Within the context of our current global crisis, this will become the difference between survivalism and community-as-mutual interdependence.

BEING WITH

It was the spring of 1985 and Kim, my wife, was squatting on a bed, groaning. The midwife was a few feet away. I sat directly in front Kim as she pushed, groaned again, then pushed even harder. Suddenly her eyes widened and she stared at me with a frightening intensity. It was a look of apprehension mixed with awe. She wanted to know if I was truly committed to the birth of this child. "Are we in this together?" she asked. I assure her we were, realizing we had just stepped over a vast precipice into something much larger than I had previously admitted.

Two minutes passed. Kim was now pushing with full intention. There was a flow and an ease as she moved rhythmically, calling forth the life within her.

Then, miraculously, the crown of a head appeared. A face: eyes scrunched, a raisin for a nose, miniature lips. Then shoulders, arms, wee little hands. A penis, knees, toes. Then suddenly there he was, fully out in the world. At that very moment, as Kai's body fully separated for the first time from Kim's, a desperate cry filled the room. Even though I was expecting his scream, I was surprised by its suddenness and its intensity. For a full thirty seconds that tiny, determined lament echoed about us as I briefly met the searching in his eyes. Through the force of his frantic wail he was letting me know that something was missing. I quickly turned him to meet his mother's outstretched arms. Quite suddenly, in the moment of his return to her embrace, his great wanting subsided. The message was unmistakable. He knew the feel and the form of the one who now held him. He had been rudely separated and again had returned home.

The next morning, as Kim slept for the first time in 27 hours, I took Kai into the living room and held him on my lap for a long time. Newborns are not supposed to be able to focus their eyes in the first several days after birth, but here we were, father and son, staring intently at each other. I reflected on Kim's request of me the previous evening, just before his birth. In that moment of vulnerability, her body wide open to pain and uncertainty, she needed to be told that she was not in this endeavor alone. In her vulnerability she was requesting to be held. Moments later our son would scream out with that exact same petition. "Hold me. Hold me. I cannot live without holding."

The eminent British pediatrician and psychoanalyst Donald Winnicott coined a term more than 50 years ago that describes our deepest psychological need. He called it *"a holding environment."* None of us, he said, can adequately live without a holding environment. In no way limited to physical touch, a holding environment is any caregiving relationship that engenders a genuine and safe experience of belonging.

We are programmed to need this holding. All babies intuitively know that they must have adequate protection and tender care; they are secure and confident only within a holding environment. In my field, thirty years of infant and child attachment research, including thousands of studies all over the world, have shown that a child will respond with trust and delight to a caregiver who provides sensitive and careful attention. Likewise, a child will respond with protest, despair and eventual detachment when such attention is not available. Kai, like every child born on the planet before him, knew—even at the moment of his birth—that he must remain in relationship at all costs.

This trust in the presence of a holding environment, this sense of inherent belonging, had been what I was missing during my dark night in 1972. Falling through space, disoriented and feeling utterly alone, I experienced what Donald Winnicott called "the primitive agonies." The antithesis of a holding environment, these agonies are primal events, usually experienced in a child's first several years of life. During these events an infant is deprived of being with another, of being held. Ideally, a securely attached child will know countless moments of being soothed, comforted, sensitively stimulated and calmed. For such a child, it's as if s/he is repeatedly dropping a pebble into a well and consistently hearing it land.

Many, if not most, children experience primitive agonies. These agonies seem to be a given for most of us. Themes of "falling forever," "not going on being," "complete isolation," "going to pieces," etc. are the stuff of the nightmares, nursery rhymes, fears and fairy tales to which all children (and adults) can relate.

Poet Robert Hass summarized our common plight on planet earth: "In this life the heart is going to be injured." In this life, every child and every adult will, to some degree, struggle with how to find and how to maintain a holding environment in the face of inevitable pain. None of us succeeds all the time.

Which brings us back to our common vulnerability and the Y2K problem. Like a time bomb waiting to be triggered, there are primitive agonies within many of us that may well come to the surface if the world falls into chaos. What can be done in the face of this sudden emerging of internal anguish? Said simply, it will become important to recognize and seek support from the larger nature of the universe; it will be essential that we find ways to turn to God.

After my work in prisons and cancer wards, after living and working for years with the residents of skid row, after my own journey into hell and out again, I have come to one central conclusion: God is the holding environment that we all seek. We are never alone for a single moment. The underlying support and the sustenance that we require is always available for the asking. We were programmed to need this holding in the same way we were programmed to need water. In both cases, what we require exists.

The value of this one simple truth cannot be overemphasized. So much of our attention and energy is taken up by the anxiety that results from not trusting. In a time of intense crisis, as the coming months and years promise to be, allowing ourselves the resource of a deepening confidence in God's active presence may make all the difference in how we respond to the adversity that will surround us.

This resource, this holding environment, includes us. It is actually very simplistic and dangerous to view God as someone outside that will swoop in and save us in our time of greatest need. I have never experienced God in this way. The difficulties we may be facing in the Year 2000 will require a very different view of God, one that includes Thomas Merton's insight into a "hidden wholeness." In a time that may require community and mutuality at a level we have never known, it will become essential to realize that we are each manifestations of the holding environment that we most seek. Our responses to the need that surrounds us will, in fact, become manifestations of God's response. Seeing ourselves as co-creators of the inventiveness and compassion required will be essential.

AN INCARNATE UNIVERSE

In order to better understand this hidden wholeness, of which we are all a part, it will be helpful to return to the moments just after the birth of my son. Kim and I were filled with awe, delight, joy and gratitude, but something else was also present . . . an unsolicited desire, a wanting, an intense and immediate urge to meet the needs of this small being.

Years later I found in the words of the thirteenth century Sufi mystic, Rumi, a wondrous description of the vast mystery we were now manifesting.

God created the child, that is, your wanting,
so that it might cry out, so that milk might come.

Cry out! Don't be stolid and silent
with your pain. Lament! And let the milk
of loving flow into you.

Thirst, yet again, had proven the existence of water. The difference between this time, for me, and my earlier solitary agony was that the playing field had just gotten much larger. This time, I was the water! In the brief moments before and after Kai's birth, it seemed that the underlying character of the universe was revealed in a new way.

I like to look at fractal geometry as a symbol of innate psychological patterns. Fractal geometry describes the recurrence and similarity of forms in nature from the microcosmic to the macrocosmic: it is like painted Russian nesting dolls, shapes and patterns in nature that appear the same whatever the scale. For example, blood vessels, tree roots and river beds all share the same structure. That which is descriptive of the smaller scale or "individual" experience can thus be understood as a manifestation of the whole.

As a psychotherapist intensely involved in the study of human attachment, and now as a parent, I was becoming aware of a "self-similarity" in every child's request for affection. At the same time, I was beginning to see a "self-similar" willingness, within myself and

In the face of thirst, I learned,
I am capable of becoming water.

within many other parents, to respond in uniquely loving ways to this request. Thus, a question came into focus. Is my personal love for Kai part of a much larger "personal" fractal? Is our common need for tender and personal presence a reflection of an intimate and personal God?

Robert Frost described love as "the irresistible desire to be irresistibly desired." Frost speaks to our innate and core need to be wanted, to be met, to be loved. And yet true affection is always a two-way street. Not only do we have the need to be loved, we also have the need to love. Whether it be between parent and child, sister and brother, friend and friend, neighbor and neighbor, or (as is often the case in times of crisis and vulnerability) stranger and stranger—there is within us a natural willingness to seek and to provide deep caring.

My son, at the moment of his birth, knew that he belonged to his mother's waiting arms. In that same moment, she knew with every fiber of her being an undeniable need to respond to his request for holding. As a psychotherapist I often listen to parents talk about their experience of being caregivers to their young children. Many of these parents describe a sense of awe about a process happening through them, a process that feels beyond their control. "She lets me know what she needs, and I want so much to meet her needs." "He is teaching me that I have an ability to love. It's an ability much bigger than I could have guessed." "She shows me my own goodness, because I want to be worthy of her trust. She has put her life in my hands. That amazes me."

The tenderness I have when I am holding my son is but one sign of the "infinite merged with the finite." The fractal of a loving relationship can also manifest in the care I experience for my friend, my neighbor, my client or someone I have never met standing on the street corner. All of these are manifestations of the boundless heart that is the nature of the universe. I am now willing to believe that in any moment of deep care and concern I am aligning and expressing . . . *being* that love within the mysterious present. In the face of thirst I am capable of becoming water.

A friend of mine recently wrote me a letter describing the anguish of her friend, a young father, who had twin newborns in the hospital fighting for their lives. "It breaks my heart and it breaks God's," she wrote. She was right, and yet I believe that her heart and the heart of God are not separate. The heart with which she deeply cares is the same heart with which God cares. We share, we love, we are all expressions of God's boundless heart. God doesn't have a fundamentally different heart. The concern she is experiencing for her friend and his children is aligned with the very nature of love. As theologian Henri Nouwen so beautifully puts it, "The most divine is captured in the most human."

"The eye with which I see God is the same eye with which God sees me," said thirteenth century Christian mystic Meister Eckhart.

St. Augustine put it another way, "There is a mutual indwelling of the One who is holding and the one who is held."

Thus—our eyes, our hands and our hearts become the living expression of that boundless heart surrrounding us all. When any of us care deeply for another, in that particular loving moment, we align with and become the *human experience* of Love . . . infinite and personal love manifesting itself in a finite and human form.

Trusting in the co-creation that can happen through us, if we will allow ourselves to become available to it, may well be one of the most important survival tools available to us in the years ahead. Trusting that the universe is actively seeking to utilize each of us as a part of the creativity and compassion required in a time of crisis, will certainly be of benefit. Not that this co-creative process will be easy. Or even fun. It seems that suffering, in a context of ongoing hardship, may well be what we will face on a daily basis for a considerable amount of time. Life is unfair, film at eleven.

WAY WILL OPEN

It is no coincidence that the most popular film of all time (and not surprisingly just in time for Y2K) is the movie *Titanic*. The irony is almost humorous. Here we are, faced with the collapse of civilization as we know it, obsessed with the sinking of this "unsinkable" monument to modern technology. We, too, find ourselves in the middle of an ocean, almost wholly dependent upon the strengths and the weaknesses of our technology. If we don't do something very quickly, this technology will apparently sink. Shit happens.

But so do mystery and miracles. Crisis, pain and suffering happen. But so does grace. If there is any way to counter the deep panic and despair that are beginning to set in for those willing to look directly at the issues surrounding Y2K, it will be centered around an understanding that resources actually flourish in times of crisis. Just as the immune system mobilizes whenever pathogens appear, so too unseen resources abound when great calamity occurs.

Over the past twenty-five years I have begun to believe in something of a spiritual law. It first emerged into my thinking about a year after my dark night of the soul. I was looking at a piece of calligraphy by the renowned artist Corita Kent and was moved by her artistic elegance and spiritual integrity. With beautiful lettering she had written the words, "To believe in God is to know that all the rules will be fair and that there will be wonderful surprises." I kept reading this quotation and puzzling over it. I jotted it down, unable to pay the several hundred dollars required to purchase the original, and carried it with me for months. Time and again I considered the words, and time and again I felt that something about them wasn't right.

In the midst of the work I was then doing with people living on skid row in Los Angeles, I was unable to accept that "all the rules will be fair." Fair just didn't seem like the word to fit the equation. What I saw on a daily basis was that terrible and grossly unfair things happen to the poor. In the five years that I worked with the Catholic Worker, making soup, collecting discarded produce and distributing it to Mexican immigrants, counseling sexual abuse survivors, providing hospitality to the homeless—it was clear that the poverty and discrimination in our country were grossly unfair.

Often there was little that we, or those we served, could do to stop the torment. Consistently taken advantage of by slum landlords and abusive police officers, hounded by zealous fundamentalists trying to save their souls, and neglected by bureaucractic city and state officials who would have made Boris Yeltsin's government look effective, the poor living on the mean streets of Los Angeles did not experience justice. Of course we were advocates for them at city hall. We took the slumlords to court. We even got ourselves arrested on occasion to uphold the right to salvage and distribute thousands of pounds of perfectly edible fruits and vegetables that were being thrown away every day by the central clearinghouse for produce in Southern California. Even so, often our only option seemed to be one of not running away in the face of our shared powerlessness. Being with. That was all we could offer.

I have come to trust this odd combination of powerlessness existing alongside a holding environment.

In the late '70s, after completing my first Zen meditation retreat, a small gathering of participants sat around talking, and a woman related the following dream: "It was the middle of the night and I

*To believe in God is to know that
every moment is being fully held,
and that there will be wonderful surprises.*

was suspended over a wide chasm, hanging by my arms as my hands
tightly gripped the metal bars of a jungle gym. Throughout the night
I hung with my hands and arms getting increasingly fatigued until I
thought I couldn't stand it for another moment. And yet I knew I
didn't dare let go, because if I did I would crash to my death on the
rocks below me. Gradually the sun began to rise and with it the first
hint of light. And with that light, I could begin to make out the shapes
and contours of the scene beneath me. What slowly became apparent
was that I had spent the entire night suspended only a few inches
above the earth. Plain, solid ground lay beneath me. In any instant I
could have let go and dropped with complete safety."

Whether we come to this knowledge at nine months or ninety
years of age, once we can trust that we are genuinely held and truly
belong, we can begin to settle into this existence and stop fighting
for our lives. When we are assured that we are fundamentally held,
that we are not alone, that unconditional love and resources are always with us, then we can withstand any pain.

Thus, as we face the crisis of Y2K, it becomes important for
each of us to find simple, sustainable and daily ways to practice an
awareness of our being held, of our never being alone for a single
moment. Then can we begin to let our weight down into the mysterious holding that enfolds us and with increasing trust allow the release of doubt, cynicism and fear.

Grace happens. I trust this simple truth. The pain we suffer
doesn't necessarily stop, the anxiety doesn't disappear, the fear and
trembling may even remain. But right there, in the midst of all the
difficulty, is the holding environment that is willing to be with us no
matter what happens. We suffer, and in the same moment live outside the suffering. We are in pain and at the same time participate in
the holding of that pain. Twenty-six years after I first saw the Corita
Kent calligraphy, I have rewritten the words: "To believe in God is
to know that every moment is being fully held, and that there will be
wonderful surprises."

The Quakers have a lovely saying, "Way will open." It is their way of trusting that something is going on beyond our current understanding, that forces are operating in this world and beyond that are working for our greatest good. If we panic and push against the river, we only make matters worse. Patience and a willingness to wait, the Quakers are telling us, are virtues that must become skills in times of difficulty. The famous Swiss psychiatrist, Carl Jung, was fascinated with the unseen processes in the universe that function outside of our consciousness. He coined a word, now quite popular, to describe this mystery. He called it "synchronicity." This idea is meant to give us something of a coat rack upon which to hang the unexpected and unexplainable events that just happen.

Since the moment I randomly picked up the book describing a woman's "dark night" that so fully paralleled my own, I began to trust that new and unforeseen possibilities are always an option. Christians call it providence and grace, Buddhists call it "the formless field of benefaction," Jung called it synchronicity. The name isn't important. In believing that change is happening, even when we have no sign of it, we midwife the conditions that allow for that change. Way will open. Eventually. Way is opening. Now. To believe in God is to know that every moment is being fully held and that there will be wonderful surprises.

Ask

The last place Thomas Merton visited in the United States prior to his untimely death in Thailand in 1968 was a monastery in northern California. In 1973, still on the mend from my experience a year earlier, I discovered this place, called Redwoods Monastery, on the Mendocino Coast above San Francisco. There I met a powerful group of women, Cistercian nuns, active in Amnesty International and a wide variety of ecological issues. These women for the most part lived a life of silence—dedication to meditation and prayer.

That first visit was profound for me because it provided living examples, models of spiritual faith, that exhibited deep compassion, social relevance and dedication to a mysterious, loving God. Over the next seven years, prior to moving to the Pacific Northwest, I often returned to this monastery to spend time on retreat.

Over that time I came to know Veronique, one of the nuns, quite well. We often talked about spiritual issues, and on one occasion I rather awkwardly wondered if she might tell me what she had come to know after her almost thirty years committed to a life of silence and prayer.

"I feel strange asking such a question, Veronique, but is there anything you could say to summarize what you have come to under-stand about God and your relationship to God?"

"That is very easy, Kent," came her quick reply, filtered through a gentle Belgian accent. "I can answer that with one simple word." She then paused, looked at me with her comfortable smile and said, "Ask."

Theologian James Carse challenges each of us when he says, "The heart is a beggar. Petition and supplication are its natural modes. Begging comes from need. If you know your need, if you do not shut your eyes to the truest longings of your heart, you will know where to take your petitions."

The privilege of our being alive, even in times of immense suf-fering, is found not within a life that is free from unmet needs, but within a life that includes inevitable pain alongside a sense of hold-ing that can support our willingness to contain both our agony and our ecstasy. In allowing ourselves to ask for the help we need, we do not necessarily get what it is that we seek. As was said at the begin-ning of these pages, an honest and open expression of vulnerability allows for fresh and unexpected possibilities. It is in this vulnerabil-ity, this full feeling of our need, that a means is opened within us to receive what is given.

Veronique said, "Ask."

But for what, specifically, do we ask? The answer, of course, is as unique as the person doing the asking. But one might be to ask for the capacity to stay open to the wisdom and creativity that is seeking to happen through us. "May the deepest and highest good be mani-fest within my actions. May the deepest and highest good be mani-fest through all beings." In addition, we will need to ask for the ca-pacity to live with gratitude for what is, including pain and adversity. "May I have the courage and the strength to accept and embrace any hardship I face. May I learn from this present experience. May I be given the capacity to make it through."

Veronique said, "Ask. And ask again."

She knew that before asking we must have some reason to trust. Therefore, we first need to ask for an ever-deepening confidence in sacred mystery. "May I trust that a relationship exists into which my deepest needs and fears can be fully revealed and fully held. May I trust this relationship into which I am increasingly putting my full weight, believing that I am known and loved and responded to. May I trust that as I realize this tender holding that surrounds me, I will be able to more fully accept life exactly as it is."

In our trusting may we all know that no matter how things appear in the present, there will always—always—be wonderful surprises. #

Kent Hoffman, a Spokane, Washington-based psychotherapist, holds a doctorate in religion. He is the former chaplain of Chapman College, and has counseled at a women's prison, in a ward for terminal cancer patients, and for five years served the poor with the Los Angeles Catholic Worker. With colleagues at Spokane's Marycliff Institute, he is pioneering a new model of parent training based on attachment theory.

I Once Was Lost...

BY JUDY LADDON

It was July 23rd, 1998, when I fell off my horse, figuratively speaking.

Like a blow to the solar plexus, I became aware that, "Y2K is for real, brought to you courtesy of your divine power source."

From the moment this book was conceived on the 26th, it took twelve days to write, gather the articles, edit, assemble and design a computer pasteup, ready for printing.

That includes the time necessary for me and Larry to experience and resolve a little marital/power conflict.

I want to elaborate on that, because it's important. Always in our past, Larry has been the moving power behind the magazine/book/investigative report efforts, and I have supported and served him. This time, as he began to state his opinions emphatically (including the caution that I shouldn't use the expression "spiritual awakening," which might turn people off, but instead something like "creative collaboration"), I said, "We need to talk." I informed him that some powerful force was moving in me, that it was unmistakable and that I needed to be in charge of this book. I wanted him to be my colleague, but I needed to be "lead editor." Would that be acceptable to him?

We were having this conversation on a hot morning, sitting beside the fish pond in our backyard. He instantly got it and said to me, "Not only will you be in charge of this project, but I will work for you. You just tell me what you want me to do." I started my new role as lead editor and boss by collapsing into tears. "I can't tell you how good it feels to have you say that," I explained. I don't think a man can understand the way women give their power away, all over the place, year after year. The symbolism of the moment was crystal clear: all the wise and quiet women who are serving their husbands, their families, their communities, their countries, need to step into their own power, come forward and lead the way out of this bizarre wilderness. And gentlemen, please quiet your voices and listen to what they have to say. It's not that women are better. We're all family; we're all equal. But given the different modus operandi of the genders in our global cultures, it will take some effort to honor that equality.

So anyway, this book was put together in less than two weeks. Granted, it was hard work. I woke up many mornings at 4 a.m., (that's what the clock says right now as I type these words into my computer), but it was done. In contrast, I've been working on a novel for over three years, it's still years from completion, and beyond that I'm hounded by doubts about whether it's any good. There's no doubt about this book. I know it to be good. The reason for this phenomenal productivity?

Two things:

1) I'm not trying to do it alone, to write it all by myself. It's truly a collaborative effort, but one driven by my fierce intuition. Most of the articles were already written. Tom Atlee had already done a phenomenal job on his web site in collecting a range of fine thinking and writing about the subject of Y2K. (And surprise! He was happy to work with me!) Each writer, as I contacted them, was pleased to participate in this project. I asked a couple of people to revise an existing script to be appropriate for this book—Jim Lord and Paul Glover—and I wondered if they could do it immediately. Yes, they said. I knew who among my friends and acquaintances I wanted to give writing assignments: Larry, of course, Kent Hoffman, Marilyn Trail. Both Kent and Marilyn were leaving town in three days. They were willing to drop what they were doing to participate. Kent called me and reported, "For three months I've been working on a book, and it's been like walking through molasses. It's so painful, the words don't come, I'm blocked. Then you call and give me this assignment and," he made a buzzing sound with his tongue, "it just pours out."

The point is, this book is an example of what we each can do in response to Y2K. If we act individually, we'll still be short of firewood come January 1, 2000, whereas if we act collectively, we can expect a miracle of abundance, inspiration and productivity.

One lesson is that the work is a grassroots effort. We can't wait for someone else to take care of us, not the government, or more capable or knowledgable experts, or the usual organizations or systems. Here's an example. On Day 6 of my ephiphany, I overnighted a book proposal to a top agent in New York and asked for her immediate review. The next day a fax rolled into my office declining the project. I blessed her for responding so quickly, and I immediately got it. We would publish this book ourselves. I know how to do it! Why do I always think I need somebody else's money or support or power?

2) The presence of the Divine. Never in my life have I felt with such certainty the presence of a divine power. And that includes a few years in the 1980s when I received "channeled" writings from an otherworldly entity, writings which now appear to be remarkably pertinent. (*Beyond the Veil*, though not currently in print in the U.S., is available in Holland, Japan, Brazil, Poland and Italy, in modest numbers.) Normally I feel a connection to a power beyond me during discrete moments: an upwelling of feeling while listening to music, or children singing, looking at a sunset, or into the eyes of my loved ones. During these strange days I feel it more obviously. I tingle with energy, and I know what I need to do next. I make plans based on that knowledge, impractical plans by my usual standards, not knowing whether the resources will show up. I just expect them to. And the daily miracles have been amazing.

Let me give an example. I was sitting in the living room earlier this week, eating a bowl of cereal as Larry and I were preparing to go inline skating on the Centennial Trail down by the Spokane River. Our daughter Katie, age 19, was joining us. "Can I talk shop for a minute?" I asked Larry. Sure. "Today I want you to drop everything and write your chapter for the book."

"Okay, but what do you have in mind? How many words?" Our usual banter.

"You'll know," I said meaningfully.

"I hate that spiritual shit."

We both were laughing when Katie pointed to the fireplace. Against the glass-doored insert fluttered a bird. I opened the door and a young robin, its breast still speckled, hopped onto the fireplace door, as bright and healthy as could be. It looked around calmly while Larry rushed to the front door and opened it. I approached the bird, my hand out. It didn't seem frightened, but when I reached to pick it up, it fluttered toward a screened window, then fell to the floor. I got the screen off, opened the window, and a moment later the bird flew to the sill, then took off into the front yard, apparently none the worse for wear.

I turned back to Larry, who had just said, "I hate that spiritual shit."

"Did you want a sign?"

"Well, yes!" he scoffed. "But that was just a *robin;* it wasn't an *eagle!*"

A sense of humor is a blessing.

In collecting these articles I didn't have time to become an instant expert on Y2K. I couldn't read very many articles but had to trust that I would be led to good ones. It started with Robert Theobald, whom I knew to be respected, Bob Stilger, whom I personally admire, Tom Atlee, a friend of Theobald and Stilger, and so on. I had to trust friends and friends of friends.

Similarly, there hasn't been time to do the kind of fact and source checking that you would insist on in good journalism. I did speak in person to all the authors (or receive e-mail permission to reprint something already on the web). And where I looked into the validity of secondary sources, they checked out.

But if members of the press review this book or use it for research, I suggest double-checking quotes and sources.

As you have noticed, there are a variety of sometimes divergent viewpoints in this collection: what to expect come January 1, 2000; whether to store food; who to blame. Readers will be able to see my bias in the most crucial aspect of this disturbing news: how to feel about it. I lean strongly towards hope, and action. I didn't feel moved to include authors saying there's nothing to worry about for the obvious reason that that viewpoint is already prevalent. Why this story is such a sleeper is beyond me.

If you fall off your horse, like I did, don't expect to be instantly popular with family and friends. This isn't delightful news, and it threatens an establishment with a vested interest in maintaining their power.

In the early '50s Dr. Alice Stewart in England warned the medical community that giving x-rays to pregnant women appeared to harm their fetuses. For her trouble she lost her position as Chair of the Department of Social Medicine at Oxford University. But she was persistent. From Birmingham University she continued her Oxford Survey of Childhood Cancer, the world's oldest cancer cohort study, and it eventually changed the paradigm of x-ray usage, saving millions of children.

We all need to be like Alice and just get on with what needs to be done.

The contributors to this book weren't able to see the entirety before it went to press. And I couldn't tell you if they will all feel proud to be included. I have shared several of the articles with Tom Atlee, who protested at my inclusion of the Thomas Merton parable at the end. He wrote:

"It is a lovely story. However, if we can't create worthwhile effects unless we are that enlightened, I think we're in real trouble.

I'm certainly not that empty, and, especially now with my sense of the importance of all this and my urge to act, I'm not likely going to progress very far towards that ideal emptiness before the clock strikes midnight (however much the Buddha and Chuang Tzu may be rooting for me to do so). The fact is, this scene is going to be a good deal messier than any of us would like, with a LOT of different agendas blowing in the wind. My focus will be partly on pushing my agenda (sustainability/resilience/transformation) and partly on creating forums (e.g., open space conferences) where diverse agendas can speak to each other and/or self-organize for more complementary effectiveness."

My reason for including the Merton piece isn't wholly clear to me. My eyes simply fell on it this week, and I knew it was perfect, not as a lofty ideal but as a reminder that we don't have to push the river, that we must depend on a greater mystery to help us. In my life I have regularly been ashamed of an urge to proselytize about some nutritional wonder or health remedy, some worthy cause or some political issue. I should know better. I hate it when somebody tries to convince me of something. "Just give me the facts quietly, and I'll make up my own mind." The parable reminds me that I don't have to yell to be heard, and that what goes on inside me is as important as what goes on out there.

As I assembled this book, I operated in my normal state of consciousness, but my own writing in it at times seemed as much channeled as anything I wrote back in the '80s. It may put off some readers, but I have to respect whatever force seized my imagination and spirit and compelled me to do this project.

THE SPECTER OF Y2K, of the collapse of our way of life, the vision of a twisted, ironic Dark Age rolling inexorably toward us to snatch away every resource we have depended upon, is nothing to be feared. On the contrary, this is a time for rejoicing. It's what we were born for. It's the earth-shattering transformation of a 10,000-year-old human experiment.

The experiment has been declared a success.

Now it's time to go home.

Humans called out, "Let us play with light and dark. Create a stage where some people can delve into extremes, portraying villains and victims, on large scale and small, an interplay of domination and submission of individuals over each other and of humanity over the earth itself.

"We want to pretend we are separate and alone. Allow us to see our own capacities! Let us imagine we wander through a wilderness abandoned by its Creator. Let us probe the depths of the human psyche and construct a cardboard world of belief in human power above the divine."

And the Great Spirit and Creator-of-All, said, "So be it!"

The whole Y2K thing has the unmistakable signature of the Divine. Yes, it was human error that created the two-digit problem that infected the cybernetic system that has grown into the foundation of our interactions. Yet how easily it could have been fixed, decades ago.

I can't help marveling at the opportunity before us. Doesn't it strike you as odd that in a culture that reveres creativity and innovation, no one predicted this? By the time the world wakes up (hopefully very soon), it will be too late to rely on the same solutions that created the problem.

Something new is needed. That's why you, dear reader, are holding this book. This is the grand adventure we've been prepared for. This is our moment to step forward with courage, faith and love, knowing finally that we can rely on firmer ground than we've ever known.

Look for miracles, and they will happen. "Build it and they will come." Take heart, have faith, and we will find greater comfort than we ever thought possible. By expecting partnership with the unseen forces that have always supported us, that give us breath, that cause our hearts to beat, something new will be born.

In a cosmic twist of the words of the Titanic's captain ("It *can* sink and it *will!*"), I say to you, "We *can* create a new world, and we *will.*" #

The Fasting of the Heart*

—By Thomas Merton

Yen Hui, the favorite disciple of Confucius, came to take leave of his Master.

"Where are you going?" asked Confucius.

"I am going to Wei."

"And what for?"

"I have heard that the Prince of Wei is a lusty full-blooded fellow and is entirely self-willed. He takes no care of his people and refuses to see any fault in himself. He pays no attention to the fact that his subjects are dying right and left. Corpses lie all over the country like hay in a field. The people are desperate. But I have heard you, Master, say that one should leave the state that is well governed and go to that which is in disorder. At the door of the physician there are plenty of sick people. I want to take this opportunity to put into practice what I have learned from you and see if I can bring about some improvement in conditions there."

"Alas!" said Confucius, "you do not realize what you are doing. You will bring disaster upon yourself. Tao has no need of your eagerness, and you will only waste your energy in your misguided efforts. Wasting your energy you will become confused and then anxious. Once anxious, you will no longer be able to help yourself. The sages of old first sought Tao in themselves, then looked to see if there was anything in others that corresponded with Tao as they knew it. But if you do not have Tao yourself, what business have you spending your time in vain efforts to bring corrupt politicians into the right path? . . . However, I suppose you must have some basis for your hope of success. How do you propose to go about it?"

Yen Hui replied: "I intend to present myself as a humble, disinterested man, seeking only to do what is right and nothing else: a completely simple and honest approach. Will this win his confi-

---

*By Thomas Merton, from THE WAY OF CHUANG TZU. Copyright © 1965 by The Abbey of Gethsemani. Reprinted by permission of New Directions Publishing Corp.

dence?"

"Certainly not," Confucius replied. "This man is convinced that he alone is right. He may pretend outwardly to take an interest in an objective standard of justice, but do not be deceived by his expression. He is not accustomed to being opposed by anyone. His way is to reassure himself that he is right by trampling on other people. If he does this with mediocre men, he will all the more certainly do it to one who presents a threat by claiming to be a man of high qualities. He will cling stubbornly to his own way. He may pretend to be interested in your talk about what is objectively right, but interiorly he will not hear you, and there will be no change whatever. You will get nowhere with this."

Yen Hui then said: "Very well. Instead of directly opposing him, I will maintain my own standards interiorly, but outwardly I will appear to yield. I will appeal to the authority of tradition and to the examples of the past. He who is interiorly uncompromising is a son of heaven just as much as any ruler. I will not rely on any teaching of my own, and will consequently have no concern about whether I am approved or not. I will eventually be recognized as perfectly disinterested and sincere. They will all come to appreciate my candor, and thus I will be an instrument of heaven in their midst.

"In this way, yielding in obedience to the prince as other men do, bowing, kneeling, prostrating myself as a servant should, I shall be accepted without blame. Then others will have confidence in me, and gradually they will make use of me, seeing that I desire only to make myself useful and to work for the good of all. Thus I will be an instrument of men.

"Meanwhile, all I have to say will be expressed in terms of ancient tradition. I will be working with the sacred tradition of the ancient sages. Though what I say may be objectively a condemnation of the prince's conduct, it will not be I who say it, but tradition itself. In this way, I will be perfectly honest, and yet not give offense. Thus I will be an instrument of tradition. Do you think I have the right approach?"

"Certainly not," said Confucius. "You have too many different plans of action, when you have not even got to know the Prince and observed his character! At best, you might get away with it and save your skin, but you will not change anything whatever. He might perhaps superficially conform to your words, but there will be no real change of heart."

Yen Hui then said: "Well, that is the best I have to offer. Will you, Master, tell me what you suggest?"

"You must *fast!*" said Confucius. "Do you know what I mean by fasting? It is not easy. But easy ways do not come from God."

"Oh," said Yen Hui, "I am used to fasting! At home we were poor. We went for months without wine or meat. That is fasting, is it not?"

"Well, you can call it 'observing a fast' if you like," said Confucius, "but it is not the fasting of the heart."

"Tell me," said Yen Hui, "what is fasting of the heart?"

Confucius replied: "The goal of fasting is inner unity. This means hearing, but not with the ear; hearing, but not with the understanding; hearing with the spirit, with your whole being. The hearing that is only in the ears is one thing. The hearing of the understanding is another. But the hearing of the spirit is not limited to any one faculty, to the ear, or to the mind. Hence it demands the emptiness of all the faculties. And when the faculties are empty, then the whole being listens. There is then a direct grasp of what is right there before you that can never be heard with the ear or understood with the mind. Fasting of the heart empties the faculties, frees you from limitation and from preoccupation. Fasting of the heart begets unity and freedom."

"I see," said Yen Hui. "What was standing in my way was my own self-awareness. If I can begin this fasting of the heart, self-awareness will vanish. Then I will be free from limitation and preoccupation! Is that what you mean?"

"Yes," said Confucius, "that's it! If you can do this, you will be able to go among men in their world without upsetting them. You will not enter into conflict with their ideal image of themselves. If they will listen, sing them a song. If not, keep silent. Don't try to break down their door. Don't try out new medicines on them. Just be there among them, because there is nothing else for you to be but one of them. Then you may have success!

"It is easy to stand still and leave no trace, but it is hard to walk without touching the ground. If you follow human methods, you can get away with deception. In the way of Tao, no deception is possible.

"You know that one can fly with wings: you have not yet learned about flying without wings. You are familiar with the wisdom of those who know, but you have not yet learned the wisdom of those who know not.

"Look at this window: it is nothing but a hole in the wall, but because of it the whole room is full of light. So when the faculties are empty, the heart is full of light. Being full of light, it becomes an influence by which others are secretly transformed." #

Acknowledgments

I'm deeply grateful to Tom Atlee for collecting such fine articles and networking with so many concerned people trying to blunt the potential damage of Y2K. Of the 17 articles appearing in this book, ten were taken from his website, and four of those he personally authored. My thanks to Robert Theobald for gently nudging me off my horse, and to John Petersen, Meg Wheatley and Myron Kellner-Rogers for allowing me to really "get it." To produce a book of this size and quality in twelve days required the speedy cooperation of people who didn't know me from Eve, plus the instant enthusiasm from friends to whom I turned to write their contributions on the spot: Kent Hoffman harnessed the energy and turned it into inspiration; Larry Shook, my dear helpmate and husband, did a superb piece of reporting and reflection while reeling from the tornado that our quiet life had turned into; Marilyn Trail saw the connections between a computer glitch and ancient prophecies. I was truly honored to be able to include William McDonough's extraordinary speech. My sister, Sue (Anne), an artist, designed the book's cover with three days' notice. And my dear mother-in-law, Dorothy Shook, who makes beautiful quilts, insisted on paying for the first printing with her personal savings.

—JUDY LADDON

Most of what is in this book came off of the World Wide Web, or came from contacts gotten through the World Wide Web. Y2K is a rapidly-evolving problem and an opportunity which changes too fast for books like this to keep up with. But not everyone has access to the Web, so we offer this book as a touchstone, a marker on the path for those who cannot follow the rapidly-unfolding story of Y2K on the Web. It is the best wisdom we were able to gather in a few weeks time, to represent this powerful moment in history. But we urge you to connect up with the Web—on your own, through your local library, or through a friend who has Internet access. We are all on this journey together, whether we want to be or not, and it behooves us to get as clear a view as we can of the road ahead and the resources available to work with.

Because of the limitations of this book, we have not been able to represent the full contributions of all of those we think are making a difference with this issue. There are some people, in particular, whose very important work should be explored by anyone interested in creative approaches to the Year 2000. Engineer Harlan Smith has been working out the details of our need to focus on preparing the "austere infrastructure" of community survival—our supplies of water, food, warmth, etc. Paul Glover and Larry Victor provide powerful visions of what we could do to transform our culture towards sustainability. Steve Davis, Leon Kappelman, John Westergaard, Ed Yardeni and others offer excellent guidance for global, national, state and local governing bodies, on how to best prepare for the coming crisis. Computer Professionals for Social Responsibility (CPSR) are helping small businesses, nonprofits, and local communities think clearly about this problem, and are also helping clarify the issues and dispel the many rumors surrounding Y2K.

And for the networking and learning needed to prepare ourselves and our communities, few resources are more valuable than The Cassandra Project and The Millennium Salons, and the listservers (e-mail conferences) run by natural grocer Cynthia Beal. Ian Wells in Lowell, MA, is only one of the many local Y2K organizers who are helping develop knowhow and models that all organizers can use. And finally we have to thank the many people who have been developing sustainable communities and technologies for decades—such as the Fellowship of Intentional Communities and the Context Institute—and the many Paul Reveres of the Y2K issue: Peter de Jager, Gary North, Ed Yourdon, Senator Robert Bennett and others. The vast network of people working on this problem gives us hope. We thank them all and, if you haven't met them yet, we encourage you to climb aboard, get acquainted, and roll up your sleeves! There's more than enough work for everyone. It is good, important work, in the company of some amazing people.

—TOM ATLEE

Cynthia Beal Notes

Workshop at the Provender Alliance's Port Townsend conference
October 3 and 4, 1998. (For food folks)

"Do you feel lucky?"

On August 15, 1997, Cynthia Beal began to research the impacts of the Millennium Bug on the Red Barn Natural Grocery in Eugene, Oregon. Since then she's gathered a lot of information, and the question marks are not decreasing. If you're wondering about this issue, and you ask "Why, at this late date, is it even a question if the power will work, or the phones will operate, or the planes will fly, or the manufacturers will produce, or the railroads will function, or the fuel will arrive, or the ports will operate, or the inventory manifests will be okay?", you'll have the appropriate frustration level to attend this workshop. If you agree not to talk about that too much, and instead discuss what we should do since this stuff is STILL in question, this may just be the workshop for you. This is NOT about fixing your computers (though we'll touch on that) - this is about what to do since other people haven't fixed theirs, and no one plans to stop eating just because the infrastructure has a convulsion or two.

Cynthia Beal is a grocer, farmer, writer and plant conservator in Lane County, Oregon. Examining potential impacts of Y2K on the Red Barn Natural Grocery, the blueberry operation at Winter Green Farm, and the Pacific Rim Medicinal Plant Conservancy have led her to a sobering analysis of the food chain, especially within the context of modern agriculture and food distribution, and the realities of small business in a global production environment.

Service on the boards of directors of a small farm financing group, a natural foods trade association, an organic farmers' cooperative, and neighborhood council work in Eugene, Oregon, over the past decade add another dimension to the questions she wishes to share with others in her search for a process that simultaneously manages risk as responsibly as possible, while building community and the tools for recovery from interruption and assistance to others in crisis.

Cynthia talks and writes as a business person and citizen whose work—attending to the needs of a safe, healthful and sustainable food supply—should continue, especially in the face of Y2K challenges, and she can share thoughts about how that might best be done within the variety of circumstances people may encounter over the next 18-24 months.

CONTACT INFO:

Cynthia Beal, PO Box 694, Eugene, Oregon 97440
541-710-1036

cabeal@efn.org
http://skymind.org

"Security is mostly a superstition. It does not exist in nature,
nor do the children of men as a whole experience it.
Avoiding danger is no safer in the long run than outright exposure.
Life is either a daring adventure or nothing.
To keep our faces toward change and behave like free spirits
in the presence of fate is strength undefeatable."

—HELEN KELLER
"Let Us Have Faith"

APPENDIX B

DACIA REID REFERENCES

Y2K BIBLIOGRAPHY

Time Bomb 2000: What the Year 2000 Computer Crisis Means to You! By Edward Yourdon & Jennifer Yourdon, Prentice Hall PTR, 1998. Fourteen chapters covering a wide range of topics including Impact on Jobs, Impact on Banking, Impact on Your Home PC and Impact on Food. Each chapter includes "Fallback Advice" for two-day, one-month, one-year and ten-year shutdowns. Very well written by this father and daughter team. Ed Yourdon is the author of 25 computer books. Top-seller at www.Amazon.com. Also available at local bookstores.

The Year 2000 Software Problem: Quantifying the Costs and Assessing the Consequences by Capers Jones, Addison Wesley, 1998. Carefully detailed presentation of what it will cost to fix the Year 2000 problem by country, by industry, by programming language and by application. Also analysis of year 2000 problems that may slip through, not fixed; cost of immediate damage and long-range recovery.

Y2K: Opportunity or Apocalypse? Video presentation and densely written compilation of other information from Prep 2000. E-mail: prepare2000@hotmail.com. The video is an intensely accurate presentation of the major Y2K concerns. Easy to order and relatively inexpensive.

Year 2000: Countdown to Calamity by Rodney Swab, Morris Publishing, Kearney, NE—(800) 650-7888. Can be purchased directly from the author by writing Rodney Swab, Box 390192, Omaha, NE 68135. Get the order form online at www.bigo.net/reswab/bkorder1.htm. Excellent, concise explanation covering the full scope of the technical problem. Text includes many useful metaphors. Foreword and Afterword reflect the author's religious views.

RELATED WEBSITES

www.Year2000.com This is a mega site with many links. Includes daily press clippings from around the world.

www.garynorth.com. His Links and Forums section arranged by categories, like banking and transportation, with over 2000 links, allows all to do their own research and draw their own conclusions. Gary North himself is uncompromising in his expectations of catastrophic problems and often draws severe criticism for being a "gloom & doomer." Still a great source of information.

www.gao.gov/y2K.htm. This site provides access to all reports and testimonies from the Government Accounting Office (GAO). Sobering.

www.y2ktimebomb.com. An online "newspaper/magazine" about Year 2000. It changes daily.

www.euy2k.com. Information on electric utility companies' progress on Y2K remediation. Also sobering.

www.state.or.us/IRMD/y2k/other.htm. Links to Y2K governmental information in every state. Also links to federal government and a few other resources.

www.uuy2k.org. The *UU Y2K Project: Unitarian Universalists Responding to the Year 2000.* Newly organized and still under development. By Rev. Dacia Reid.

"In Betweenness" from *To Whom It May Concern*
By Rev. Richard S. Gilbert

We live in betweenness:
In between festivals of gratitude and joy,
In between seasons of contrasting color,
Between floods of brightness
And seas of whiteness.
We live in betweenness:
On a remote island outpost in fathomless space,
Between stars and moons and planets and void,
Surrounded by meteors, comets, rays and nothingness
In which there is no right or left, up or down,
Only betweenness.
We live in betweenness:
Not quite atop apex of joy,
Or in nether of sorrow,
Rather, in the moving space between,
Uncertain of our location.
We live in betweenness:
Walking from city of birth to death,
Hoping along the way
To see something of beauty,
To touch hands with those we love,
To give more than we get,
To make some sense of it all.
We live in betweenness.

Endnotes

1. "Y2K for Scoffers" by Kal Gronvall of Investments Rarities, Incorporated, in Minneapolis, MN. This is an unpublished paper.

2. "The Amount of Change Required," page 3 of Year 2000 Testing: a white paper Version 2.0, MatriDigm Corporation, 1997.
http://www.matridirmusa.com/year2000.htm. See also "Table 4.4: Sample CO-BOL Application Showing Sizes of Code Divisions", The Year 2000 Software Problem: Quantifying the Costs and Assessing the Consequences by Capers Jones, page 52. Addison-Wesley, November 1997.

3. "What We Found Was Terrifying says Bank Boston's Chief Technology Officer." Year 2000 Industry, 3/10/97. http://www.y2ktimebomb.com/. Industry/Banking/bnkbost9711.htm

4. "The IRS is taxed by Y2K", PC Week, 4/3/98.
http://www.zdnet.com/dontent/pcwk/1514/302544.html And "Countdown to Chaos: Preparing for 2000. An interview with Ed Yourdon." CBN News Archives, 3/23/98. http://www.cbn.org/news/stories/980323.asp. See also "Don't Bug Me When I'm Working" by Declan from Afternoon Line with Jonathan Gregg via Netly News: Afternoon Line, 5/1/98. http://cgi.pathfinder.com/netly/afternoon/0,1012,1954,00.html

5. IRS chief says Y2K fixes must come before reform." GovEXEC.com, "Daily

Briefing", 4/16/98 by Stephen Norton and Erica Cranston, Congress Daily. http://www.govexec.com/dailyfed/0498/041698tl.htm

6. Embedded Systems & the Year 2000 Problem: The "Other" Year 2000 Problem. By Mark A. Frautschi, Department of Physics & Astronomy at Johns Hopkins University, Baltimore, MD. 3/31/98 http://tmn.com~doug/frautschi.htm And also, "Countdown to Chaos: Preparing for 2000. An interview with Ed Yourdon." See endnote #4

7. "How to Deal With The Bug: One Company's Story," by Stephen Baker, AFR Net Services, Financial Review, "Surveys" 4/20/98. Details the steps taken by Medical Mutual of Ohio. Http://www.afr.com.au/contnet/980420/survey/survey18.html

8. Senate Banking, Housing and Urban Affairs Committee: Subcommittee on Financial Services and Technology: Oversight Hearing on Financial Institutions and the Year 2000 Problem. Prepared Testimony of David Iacino, Senior Manager, Bank of Boston, N.A., 7/10/97. http://www.senate.gov/~banking/97_07hrg/071097/witness/iacino.htm OR "The Implications of the Year 2000 Computer Problem: Prepared Testimony of Mr. David M. Iacino, Senior Manager, Millennium Project, Bank Boston, 2/17/98." Senate Banking, Housing & Urban Affairs Committee: Field Hearing— The Implications of the Year 2000 Computer Problem. http://www.senate.gov/~banking/98_02hrg/021798/witness/iacino.htm

9. "Y2K Ripple Effect" by Stephanie Neil, PC Week, 4/10/98. http://www.zdnet.com/zdnn/content/pcwk/1515/306151.html

10. "70% of Asian business expected to suffer or fail: Unisys Y2K expert foresees massive social implications." By Nick Wilgus, Bangkok Post, "Database", 2/4/98. An interview with Unisys expert Phillip Dodd.

11. "Big 3 fight 2000 bug in forced upgrade: Suppliers' computers a worry to car makers." By automotive writer, Rachel Konrad, Detroit Free Press, 4/23/98. http://www.auto.com/industry/qbug23.htm

12. "CIO Szygenda Says: GM's Problems are Catastrophic." Comp.software.year-2000 Newsgroup, 4/17/98

13. Embedded Systems & the Year 2000 Problem: The "Other" Year 2000 Problem. By Mark A. Frautschi. See endnote #6.

14. "Location, Location . . . Location?: Realtors worry about Y2K embedded systems." By Declan McCullagh, Washington DC. The Netly News, "Afternoon Line", 4/27/98. http://egi.pathfinder.com/netly/afternoon/0%2c1012%c1932%2c00.html

15. "Why Is Y2K So Hard to Solve? The Metaphor of the Hong Kong Y2K Flu," Time Bomb 2000! By Edward Yourdon and Jennifer Yourdon, 1/6/98. http://www.yourdon.com/books/fallback/CH00/Hkflu.html

16. "Real-Life Examples of Date Related Problems for Electric Utilities," EUYZK.COM: Electric Utilities and Year 2000. Source for Hawaiian Electric Company—staffer e-mail, 10/31/97. http://www.euy2k.com/realife.htm See also: "Florida Power & Light Y2K Website." Entry dated 4/17/98 cites 1% of renovations completed. http://www.fpl.com/thml/2000_emb.htm Posted by Rick Cowles, a programmer with 17 years experience in electric utilities, e-mail: rcowles@waterw.com at comp.software.year-2000.

17. "Countdown to Chaos: Preparing for 2000. An interview with Ed Yourdon." See endnote #4

18. "How Y2K could kill a town: Tests Reveal Potential Catastrophe." Sun Herald of Australia, 4/26/98. http://www.garynort.com/y2k/detail_.cfm/1452

19. "ED VS. ED, on the potential for computer problems in the Year 2000." Wall Street Journal, 4/30/98.

20. "Pulling the Plug: Some Firms, Let Down By Costly Computers, Opt to

'De-Engineer' " by Bernard Wysoki, Jr., Wall Street Journal, 4/30/98. Note: Peter de Jager estimates that 86% of all (software) projects are delivered late. See "NZ claims of Y2K safety 'unjustified.'" By Phil Jones in NZ InfoTech Weekly, 4/27/98. http://www.infotech.co.nz/april_27/noy2k.html

21. "Companies surge while Year 2000 looms." Enterprise, Brockton, MA, page A11, 4/30/98, reprinted from the Raleigh News & Observer, Raleigh, NC.

22. "Blair warns of economic chaos unless millennium bug is cured." By David Parsley, The Sunday Times: Business, 3/29/98 (London). http://www.sundaytimes.co.uk/news/pages/sti/9.../stibusnws01022.html?173362. And "Millennium bug can't be stopped, says expert," by Robert Uhlig, Technology Correspondent, UK News: Electronic Telegraph, Issue 1036, 3/27/98. http://telegraph.co.uk/et?ac=00014032670927&pg=/et/98/3/27/nmil27.html3/27/98

23. "Millennium Bug boss fears chaos," The Australian, 3/3/98 by Brad Howarth. http://www.theaustralian.com.au/techno/4348121.htm AND "Civil defence alert over 2000 bug, The Trading Room News, "Financial Review", by Beverley Head and Emma Connors, 4/20/98. AFR Net Services. http://www.afr.com.au/content/980420/news/news5.html

24. "Bennett to lead 'millennium bug' battle: But it may be to late to keep computers sane." Desert News—"Web Extra" by Washington Correspondent, Lee Davidson, 4/29/98. http://www.desnews.com/cit/ud0lkggl.htm AND "Senator says agencies could get 'significant appropriations' for Y2K" by Grad Bass, Federal Computer Week, 4/28/98. http://www.fcw.com/pubs/fcw/1998/0427/web-y2Kmoney-4-28-1998.html

25. "Y2K for Scoffers" see endnote #1

26. "Y2K, Utilities, and the Titanic." By Roleigh Martin, Year 2000 Technology, March 5, 1998. http://www.y2ktimebomb.com/Computech?Issues/mrtn9809iv.htm

27. "Yardeni Gains No Supporters." By Brian Milner in Canada's Globe & Mail, 4/27/98. http://www.theglobeandmail.com/docs/news/19980427/ROBFront/ryear.html

28. "Yardeni Gains No Supporters." See endnote #27.

29. "The World According to Adam: PBS Host Adam Smith simplifies the stock market, world trade, the Year 2000 problem & then goes to the opera." By Martin Mayer in *Modern Maturity*, May-June, 1998, Volume 41W Number 3. Published by The American Association of Retired People, (AARP).

30. "Is your pacemaker ready for 2000? Your hospital hopes answer is 'Yes'." By Jane-Ellen Robinet, Pittsburgh Business Times, 4/27/98. http://www.amcity.com.pittsburgh/stories/042798/focus3.html

Additional copies of *AWAKENING: The Upside of Y2K* can be
obtained for $10 per single book, plus $2 postage and handling,
from the publisher (volume discounts available):

The Printed Word
4327 S. Perry Street
Spokane, WA 99203, USA
(509) 624-3177
Also available through Amazon.com